The Incredible Ways

of

Parenting

You Always Wanted to Know

The ultimate guide to raising a child step by step and what every parent should do in different situations as proven by science and experience

JOY NZAMWITA UWANZIGA

A BOOK FOR EVERY PARENT AND GUARDIAN, ESPECIALLY THE GREAT ONES

TABLE OF CONTENTS

DISCLAIMER i

DEDICATION ii

INTRODUCTION v

    Having a child 1

PARENTING 3

    Parents have a twofold influence 4

    Parenting Styles 6

    Infants and Toddlers 8

DISCIPLINING A CHILD 11

    Prevention 12

    Discipline and Control 13

PARENTS FROM DIFFERENT CULTURES 15

THE ROLE OF A MOTHER 19

    Qualities of a good Mother 20

OCCUPY YOUR CHILDREN 24

    Children and Play 25

    Benefits of Play 25

    Types of Play 27

    Outside influences 30

    Television, cell phones and other tablets 30

Books 32

MISTAKES PARENTS OFTEN MAKE 40

RELATIONSHIPS & CHILDREN 46

WAYS TO IMPROVE A YOUNG CHILD'S BEHAVIOR 48

Be a strong Moral Example 50

Reflect on the behaviors' effects 53

Be Consistent in Your Behavior 53

SELF-ESTEEM AND CHILDREN 55

Advantage of a Healthy Self-Esteem 57

How to foster Self-Esteem in a Child 58

ENCOURAGE CHILDREN TO EXPRESS THEIR FEELINGS 63

TEACH THE CHILD TO THINK HIGHLY OF HIMSELF 64

HELP YOUR CHILD TO BE MORE ORGANIZED 67

Make him familiar with Stories of Great People 70

TEACH YOUR CHILDREN TO TAKE GOOD CARE OF THEIR BODIES 74

INTIMATE RELATIONSHIPS 78

COUNSEL YOUR CHILDREN 80

PROVIDE A POSITIVE EMOTIONAL CLIMATE 81

TEENS AND SCHOOL 83

Apply School to the "Real World" 84

Adolescents 84

PRIVACY AND SECRECY 86

SESRETIVE CHILDREN 90

Help your child open up to you 91

DEFIANT CHILD 95

RUDENESS AND DISRESPECT 97

BULLYING 100

RUN AWAY 104

HELP YOUR TEENAGERS TO HAVE WHOLESOME SOCIAL EXPERIENCES 106

    Prepare your teenagers for the changes that will accompany puberty 107

    Girl's First Menstruation 108

    Teenagers desires for physical intimacy 111

GOING OUT 113

TEACHING CHILDREN ABOUT SEX 115

COURTSHIP AND MARRIAGE 120

    Advice to a daughter that is getting married 121

    Advice to a son that is getting married 122

    Advice to a daughter or a son that is getting married 124

PARENTS' WRONG ADVICE 131

WHEN A COUPLE BECOMES THREE 134

REFERENCES 139

DISCLAIMER

No part of this book may be reproduced or transmitted in any form or by any means, electronic or mechanical, including photocopying, recording or by any information storage and retrieval system, without written permission from the author.

The methods/steps/procedures described within this book are the author's personal thoughts. They are not intended to be a definitive set of instructions for this subject matter. You may discover there are other methods and materials to accomplish the same end result.

Behind every young child who believes in himself, is a parent who believed first,

-Matthew Jacobson, blogger

DEDICATION

I would like to dedicate this book to you dear parents and guardians. The highest purpose of any parent is to bless her/his children. Experience does teach valuable lessons. As a result of your experiences, you can bless your children by teaching them. Our time on earth is brief; there are lessons to be learned. Each precious day, another page is turned. Every chapter full of memories, times of joy and tears, through every passing year.

I dedicate it to you dear readers raising a child, and maybe you (or someone close to you) lost a child or parents in any way, at any stage. I know you would give every ounce of you to save every ounce of them, one thousand times over.

One of life's most painful losses is that of an unborn child. Miscarriages cause a pain that is unfamiliar to most and understood by few. Parents feel a strong and natural love for their unborn child and to lose their little one to death before even having a chance at life can seem unfair, cruel even.

Parents are left to wonder what might have been and a pair of empty arms can seem emptier than ever before.

Losing a child or a parent can cause pain that no one will ever understand. You wish for nothing more than just one more day with that loved one, for you would give it all. No one will ever know quite how you feel inside…no farewell, no further instruction, maybe dad didn't even disclose where the will was (if there was one). I can imagine the drama and confusion. You see things all the time that makes your mind going back to that exact moment and right there alone on the cold floor, you encounter a special moment of what life was like then. Keep her/his memory alive here forever, and someday be everything s/he hoped you would.

I would also like to dedicate this book to couples, especially the newlyweds. Finding the person who brings out the best in you and stands beside you at your worst is a key. The wedding is one day, the marriage is for the rest of your life together (unless you divorce). A good marriage is made. It doesn't just fall off the pages of a romance novel. Life will change, but, eventually, you will figure out what works for you and how to sneak in romance again.

Last but not least, I dedicate this book with a big "thank you" to my husband and children. I've been so lucky to have you as my conduit of strength to unleash a better version of me.

I hope that one day you can read this book and understand why I spent so much time on it. I would like to thank my family, including my in-laws, for the love and support, for standing beside me throughout my career and my writing endeavors. Much love and respect!

Happy reading everyone!

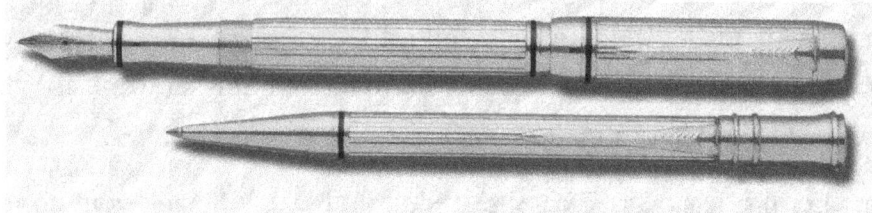

INTRODUCTION

There are many parents out there who would give anything to have a peaceful and quiet home. Whether you are single, happily married or somewhere in between, your quest for a more efficient parenting will take time. We all wish to give our children stability for life. You may not know what your child will be, but it always gives peace of mind knowing that your child is well equipped should the unthinkable happen. Some of you may think it's too late and too hard at your current stage of parenting. Always remember, it is never too late to fix the mistakes, and furthermore, you have every chance now to do right by your children.

Behaviors that a person has learned by example during early formative years have a powerful influence on his actions for the rest of his life. Parents have the influence to set children on a course that is likely to persuade them through each succeeding stage of their development. Through personal agency, children may later change the consequences of a good or bad example, but they will respond most often according to the example they observed in their homes.

As you study and apply the truths in this parental guide, do not become discouraged if your children do not respond in the way you would like them to.

Do not become discouraged when you meet with difficulty in helping your children apply these principles. Perfection does not come immediately. Be kind to yourselves as you and your children struggle toward perfection while sometimes falling short.

This book is a product of my extensive research and my personal experience as a mother. It serves its purpose well to all the parents and to the parents-to-be whom we call, 'millennials.' Being a parent and raising our angels are so sweet to think, yet difficult to fulfill. My work allows us to learn from the experts and equip ourselves with the scenarios that can be harrowing for new parents or to the ones who need further learning support.

It is divided into different categories, according to the child's stage, starting by early days. Training a child takes time and no parent should expect that after a year or some years of training, the job will be done.

Many parents leave the job to teachers and society, but it's our job first as parents. Providing the proper type of training is the main duty of the parents. Every child needs to be taught the right things, for he/she is not born with that awareness. By teaching your children the right thing, they will then have the basis they need to build up proper, loving, adventurous, and thrilling relationships in the future.

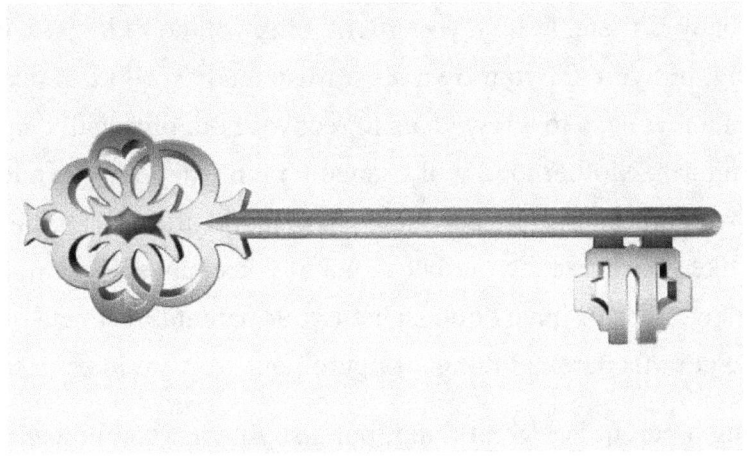

Having a child

Babies don't come with a manual. The pain may be worse or less than anticipated, labour might take minutes or days, and your long-planned vaginal delivery may turn into a caesarean. The only certainty is that you will find the strength and endurance to handle whatever comes. Once the baby is there, at first, you might think you don't know what you are doing, but you are your own most trusted advisor. It can take anything from a few days to a few years to recover both physically and mentally from birth. Motherhood will change you in weird and wonderful ways. No woman can predict how she will respond after giving birth, and it's not like you can send your baby back if you change your mind. Whether you love kids or have doubts about your parental instincts or think you have got this parental thing all figured out, you are in for a surprise.

Being a parent is a great thing, but also, having a child can sometimes be overwhelming. In other words, **prepare yourself**: Expect to spend the next couple of years watching that little crawler-walker-runner's every move!

There are times (especially mothers) when you may want to hide in your bathroom because you need that quiet for a minute, while tears roll down your cheeks.

Those times you feel so tired and feel like you can no longer continue and would do anything to lie down and get the rest you need. You may also find yourself crying on the sofa after you shouted to your children for an insignificant thing and now feel guilty and unworthy! You are not alone. It is a very difficult and crazy phase of life that most parents out there go through. We do not always talk about that, but it's hard and it's difficult in many different ways. There would be days when you will fill you need a break from your child but the moment they are out of your sight, you miss them.

Eating out is also a whole new experience. There is food on the floor to feel guilty about, crayons rolling off the table, and the angry-looking fellow dinners (at least in your mind) to deal with. And if you manage to get out for a date night alone with your significant other, you will probably spend all of the time talking or worrying about your child. Raising a child can have its challenges, but you should never give up, even in difficult times. It is definitely a time-consuming labor of love, but all in all, it will be worth it and leads to cherished memories of your little ones.

PARENTING

You may be an intelligent parent, but intelligence alone cannot guide a person to be good or moral, rather it can mislead or even destroy its possessor. There are as many parenting styles as there are children. You can't tell which style will definitely work, until your child develops his or her own personality. You keep going through phases in your own life which keeps changing your attitude and parenting style. It's a constant learning process for you as well, you keep making mistakes and learn from them. It's a trial-and- error methodology. Both parent and child keep going through these transitions and adjusting their relationship according to them. To say the least, being a parent is a position of extreme responsibility and accountability, especially for mothers. I never expected my husband to take an equal load in bringing up our children simply because he is the breadwinner who has to be out of the house. What I do expect is that he supports me, fills in the gaps and lends me a hand where needed and is always ready and willing to spend time with our children whenever he can. It may be old fashioned but I think, it is essential to bring up children respecting their father as the head of the family.

Same father who rolls on the grass with them will discipline them if he has to. It is also good to have the same goals and aim as partners while bringing up the children. Even if we have minor differences me and my husband in a given situation when dealing with a child, we have an agreement never to question each other's decision in front of the child. As far as the children see, we are always united in our sentiment.

This is important for the children so they learn to accept the decision of both parents without always thinking that they can get a different ruling if they went to the other parent.

Parents have a twofold influence

Through inheritance: Many characteristics are passed on from the genes of the parents to the children. These genes could pass on characteristics of grandparents and ancestors of the parents. Families share many qualities in common, and of inheritance cannot be overlooked. Physical and the mental traits are passed on.

The physical appearance of the child, his intelligence, his health or the lack of it sometimes are a result of inheritance.

Through contact: The first contact the child has with the mother is in the womb. This period of time is also having an effect on the child. The physical health of the womb and the emotional health of the mother during pregnancy plays an important role.

The most important training however, is done during the years the child spends with the parent. They are his first teachers as they give him awareness, a world view which will always color his thoughts and opinions. Many great aspirations, courageous behavior, noble manners as well as crooked personalities have been formed as an effect of parents.

The first home a child knows should be a source of love and respect for him, a place that has order and arrangement. When a child feels secure and safe in his home and assured of the love of his parents, he can begin to develop mentally and emotionally. Although it is true that children inherit traits such as shyness, fear, etc., it is not true that these cannot be changed. A parent can help a child overcome certain characteristics that could hamper his progress in life. Parents need first to assess what negative traits are present in the child, and then plan how to overcome them. Useful tactics may include discussions with child, reading or narrating stories where people overcome these behaviors and encouraging the child to decrease the trait.

So, for example, a shy child could be helped by being encouraged to mingle with others. In the beginning this could be with a small group of people, or people he is comfortable with. The child could be taught what to say, and how to control the fear to speak among others. Slowly the child will learn to overcome the shyness, or at least not allow it to control his life.

Life is of great value. It is good to help a child deal with disappointment and failure, to prevent him from being egoist and selfish. Many children these days feel the world should be at their feet, and their needs should be met on demand. Even when possible, it is wrong to give a child all he wants for it will create a personality that cannot bear denial.

Parents differ. Some parents believe that children will grow up and learn for themselves. It is unnecessary to burden them in their childhood years. Others think it is proper to expect children to be like adults, quick to understand what is right and quicker to obey. The correct view is in between. Children are not adults and need to be encouraged and guided. The important thing is to continue the training and realize that it has an effect on the child, even if not immediate.

Parenting Styles

Every parent is different. And often, one of the biggest differences is between generations, and that may be the reason why moms often struggle to get family members to respect their parenting choices on everything from foods to bedtimes to discipline. You may have grown up getting spanked but you don't want to use corporal punishment. Getting your family used to your parenting ideas early on can make it easier for them to accept your rules, and the family members will get to treat your kid(s) as you would. It's easy to quickly get emotional when it comes to opposition to your parenting choices but do your best to remain calm and use facts to enforce your decisions. Study up on your parenting style so that you have succinct and educated responses ready when your family begins to suggest you are doing something wrong. An intelligent and well-spoken reason is harder to fight.

It can be tempting to tell your family that they are not going to see your child until they conform to your choices, but unless their choices are truly abusive, causing such a large rift isn't the best way to solve your issues.

Using threats should only be a last resort when everything else has failed and your child's safety is in question.

Letting your family have a win sometimes will help foster good feelings. Showing that you can be flexible will help them give in sometimes, too.

Families have a lot of history, and not all of it is good. Avoid telling them that they are wrong or make bad decisions. Focus on your choices and why you are making them. Make it about you and not them. Be firm but polite and try not to bring up old hurt feelings as examples of why you are not doing things their way. Some families are rigid and will have trouble with change. If your family doesn't approve of your choices, they are probably going to offer advice and opinions on how you should really be doing things. Try to understand that they think they are helping. Listen to what they have to say but feel fine about not actually using their methods. Sometimes, family members just need to think they have got a say in how you are doing things. Always remember: You are the parent. The final say is *yours*. What you want for your child is up to you and your spouse, and nobody else. Don't be afraid to stand up for yourself when you need to. Lead by example, using your parenting style whenever and wherever you can.

If there are other small children in your family, ask if it's fine to try your techniques with them, too. If not, be certain to respect their parenting choices the same way you want them to respect yours.

Infants and Toddlers

I strongly believe that the key to raising responsible, positive and productive children is to start at a very young age, to teach them the value of living by the rules and teach them to have the consciousness and tools to make good choices on their own.

If you do not start at a very young age, you can lose control of your child very quickly. If you want a plant to grow straight without bends or to grow in the direction you want, you work on it when it's still a young plant, before it gets hard. Children have many things to learn during this period as their minds are active and ready to take on new things.

Male and female roles are an important part of this stage. Boys want to be accepted by their fathers and by other boys. Girls identify with their mothers and other girls.

There is an oft-quoted African saying which goes like "It takes a village to raise a child, and a community to keep the parents."

Furthering the idea that it takes a village to raise a child, it's not uncommon in African communities for children to live for brief periods with families that are not their own. There is an understanding that sometimes a parent is overburdened and can't be the best possible parent at the time, so friends or family take in the children for the time being, and the favor is usually returned when the tables have turned.

Since extended family and friends play a large role in raising children, they also play a large role in disciplining children. In many African countries, children are given a lot of responsibility at a very young age, tending to housework and even taking on jobs that bring family income. In many African households, if a child involves herself in things and gets in trouble, she not only has to answer to her parents, but also to her grandparents, aunties, uncles and so on. That probably gives a child a bit more motivation to behave.

Parenting young children should have few expectations in terms of behavior and acquisition of knowledge due to the cognitive limitation at this age. This does not mean that children should be allowed to run about and do as they please; they still require guidelines and boundaries.

What it does mean is that care should be taken regarding the methods that are used to raise children and the values that are instilled from the very beginning.

Play should be the primary emphasis during this time in a child's life since this is the means through which they gain an understanding of the world around them. Pretend or imaginative play is the most common type of play during this stage and this directly impacts cognitive, social, and psychological development. Children will often imitate the behavior of adults or other children around them in their play, which is their way of preparing for their particular roles in life. Girls will most often imitate their mother, and boys will follow in the footsteps of their father. You will see girls playing with dolls, dressing and feeding them. Boys in more rough-and tumble physical. These gender roles develop at an early age. It's never too early to stimulate your children's mind, be it through listening to you talking and telling stories books, counting biscuits, smelling onions while you are cooking etc. Start from the time the child is in your womb because the fetus can hear. Yes, Science has proven that many times.

The relationships that you build with your children during their early years will have a tremendous influence on the way they feel later about developing their own intimate relationships. While your children are very young, you can both show and teach them the value of loving and being loved.

They are moving from a world of immediate gratification to a world of rules, memories of the past, and wishes for the future. They develop social and speech skills.

From a relatively few family-controlled relationships, they enter into an ever-widening circle of playmates in the neighborhood and in school. They learn in a very significant way about their bodies, about social and emotional relationships.

DISCIPLINING A CHILD

A disciplined child has a much better chance of success than a child who lacks discipline. Discipline is a sign of apprehension and love from parents. It brings with it a safety and sense of belonging. Disciplining young children can be challenging for parents, especially when their children's behaviors are inappropriate. As a parent, you have the ability to help your child learn how to begin to control himself. Help your child through each phase of his life with loving discipline, by teaching him to practice good behavior. Disciplining a young child is never easy, but as the saying goes, "it is indeed easier to build strong children than to repair broken men." It takes time, effort and energy, which can all be in short supply when you are managing a career and dozens of other day to day activities parents face especially mothers.

A mother is a coach and tutor, involved in the numberless trials, errors, and successes of this developmental period. The father, on the other hand, comes home from his employment and tends to interrupt the routine. Often, he interrupts with play, sometimes with duties, and on occasion with discipline.

A good father comes home with encouragement and approval for what the mother and children have done that day; a bad one brings tension, fear and no second chances but perfection in everything at first attempt.

Prevention

The saying "Prevention is the best medicine" is true not only in the medical field, but there are many steps that parents can take to prevent misbehavior and avoid the disruption that this can cause within family. First of all, children need predictability, structure and guidelines because this gives them a sense of security and feeling that there is order and balance in the world. When this is present they are less likely to feel anxious or stressed which in turn, will decrease the likelihood of inappropriate behavior.

Children will sometimes act chaotic if they are in a chaotic environment. Sometimes the reason for misbehavior is to gain attention from a parent or other adults. A defining feature of being human is the need for social contact, approval, and attention that is already present at birth. When parents fulfill this need adequately, a child will feel content and be more likely to engage in solitary play. If a child is not able to obtain attention through positive behavior, he or she may utilize negative behavior for this purpose.

Parents can fulfill this need by spending quality time with their child (e.g.: talking, playing, reading, enjoying nature, and much more). Quality time is often more important than quantity.

It is important to realize that within these general guidelines there are about as many ways to parent as there are parents. Parents need to take into consideration the unique personalities, dispositions, and gifts of each child when deciding upon a particular approach. What may work with one child may not necessarily be effective with another.

Discipline and Control

Many parents agree that control is necessary, but they are not sure of exactly what should be controlled, and how much of a child's life should the parents' control.

It is the right of every child to be disciplined by wise and reasonable parents. A parent uses control and discipline to guide the child. Without discipline, human beings are prone to wrongdoing. A child is especially vulnerable to such tendencies for he lacks the wisdom and maturity of an adult. To follow what is right, morally and logically, requires a firm will. This does not come automatically to a child but can be developed through discipline.

A good home has certain rules that the children must follow. Children feel better when they know they are expected to follow certain guidelines in their life. Not only does life become more organized, but they are also freed from the burden of making decisions for themselves when not really in a position to do so. Although they may outwardly resent it, all children need some discipline to feel secure in life.

Effective discipline ensures that the child not only recognize why her behavior was wrong but also knows what to do to make it right next time.

Using the right kind of questions helps kids expand their ability to take another person's perspective and understand the consequences of their behavior. So, help your child reflect: "Was that the right thing to do? What should I do next time?" That way, your child learns from his mistakes and grows morally.

Discipline and control are not the same as dictatorship. Good parents take into consideration the age and understanding of the child, his circumstances, and other relative factors. Rules are then made accordingly. Sometimes the child's wishes are considered and a compromise is made. There is certain flexibility rather than rigid adherence to the rules. However, there is no doubt that parents are expected to remain in control, to make sure the children follow certain etiquette in behavior rather than a chaotic "do as you please" attitude.

PARENTS FROM DIFFERENT CULTURES

A husband may be coming from Asia and a wife from Europe or Africa. They may often have differences in the way they raise their children. Many couples in multicultural relationships have faced similar issues when parenting.

There are those cultures who adhere to a more traditional style of parenting while others don't.

Take a look at how some of the Parenting Philosophies stack up:

Mother's role

In one culture: The mother is the person responsible for running the family. She is expected to put aside her own needs for the good of the family.

In another culture: The mother must assume her role, even if she delegates tasks in order to combine her personal life with her family life.

Father's role

In one culture: The father serves as the head of the family. He personifies authority and often inspires fear. He doesn't worry about preparing meals or dealing with any issue relating to the children, unless it concerns money such as school fees, or if they are sick or they need to be punished, and that's when he intervenes.

In another culture: The father works in tandem with the mother in terms of raising their children. He is involved with discipline and making sure rules are respected. He also helps out with bedtime, games, family outings, and homework.

Grandparents and extended family's role

In one culture: Grandparents take a leading role in their grandchildren's way of living. They are concerned with their care and well-being. The extended family usually takes over, especially young women in the family.

In another culture: The grandparents are an occasional source of help and only in case of a specific need.

Otherwise, hire unrelated people, especially professionals to care for the little ones.

According to the child's gender

In one culture: Boys are less encouraged to do housework. They have more freedom to get out and play. Parents pay more attention to their success in high schools.

In another culture: Girls and boys are brought up in a more similar way. They have the same duties and granted the same freedom. Boys are encouraged to express their emotions as well as girls.

Sleeping and eating

In one culture: The child is allowed to sleep when he wants, but mealtimes are strictly observed. Meals are eaten with the entire family when everyone is present.

In another culture: Sometimes the entire family shares the same meal according to age, but there is a time when children have their meal before the adults and have a lot of control over what they eat. Adults oversee food choices to ensure balance and nutrition.

Parents' role

In one culture: Parents' guide their children and try to help them avoid mistakes. A strong focus on ethics is ingrained so that children may become productive members of the family.

In another culture: Children's aptitudes and talents are to be developed, and both parents must help them to sharpen their critical faculties and their aptitudes to make their own decisions. It's common to question oneself and to be helped by professionals in order to find one's way as a parent.

Rules and punishment

In one culture: There are no set of rules to dictate children's behavior. The child may be given verbal warnings or be spanked, so he understands he must not repeat his actions.

In another culture: It's very important to establish and to explain rules. It is even better to negotiate with a child than for them to receive a spanking. Talking and working through conflict is encouraged.

Importance given to emotional health

In one culture: It is believed that showing too much emotion can hinder a parent's ability to assert control over their children and can result in a lack of respect for the parents' authority.

In another culture: The father and the mother openly show their affection, give compliments to their child and place great value on the child in hope of building their self-confidence.

Importance given to the child's stimulation

In one culture: It is not considered productive to stimulate a child's curiosity at a young age. Hygiene, clothing, and food are more important than intellectual awakening.

In another culture: Children are stimulated as soon as possible. Parents always look for ways to develop their creativity and open their minds.

THE ROLE OF A MOTHER

Every society is made up of blocks of family units. The stronger each block is, the stronger the structure of the society. Families are thus the building blocks upon which rests the fate of society. For the development of good families, the mother plays a vital role. Many women today have aspirations of progress in their careers, and degrees in various fields. However, it is indisputable that the most important achievement of a mother is the raising of sensible, virtuous children who will then move on to build other strong blocks for society.

It has been said that it is easy to bear children but it is difficult to raise them well. In that lies the challenge for all mothers. Our mothers may have raised us in a way we think it a traditional one. They probably did the best they could give their circumstances and prevailing advice of the times. I remember once hearing a grandmother say to a mother, "I was a good mother to you, I followed exactly the schedule the doctor gave me." This new mother felt that some of her present problems stemmed from the rigid scheduling that she endured when she was a baby. She was determined to learn to read her baby's cues.

I reminded her not to blame her own mother because the prevailing parenting practice at the time was to follow the "experts" advice on child-rearing. The current mother, however, is more comfortable becoming the expert on her own child.

For you who is reading this right now: it is the right of your mother that you should appreciate that she carried you (in her womb) the way nobody carries anybody, she fed you the fruits of her heart which nobody feeds anybody. She protected you (during pregnancy) with her ears, eyes, hands, legs, limbs, etc. in other words, her whole being, gladly, cheerfully, carefully, suffering patiently all the worries, pains, difficulties and sorrows.

Till the hand of God removed you from her and brought you into this world, then she was most happy feeding you while forgetting her own hunger, wrapping and dressing you up even if sometimes herself had no clothes, giving you milk and water not caring for her own thirst, keeping you in the shade even if she had to suffer from the scorching heat of the sun, giving you every comfort with her own hardships, lulling you to sleep while keeping herself awake. Thank her if you still have one!

No one should replace her in the life of her children. She is so unique of course if she has been a good mother, with outstanding qualities.

Qualities of a good Mother

1. A deep love for her children

A mother's love is unmatched. Whether young or old, healthy or handicapped, troublesome or obedient, the child is still beloved to the mother. This love may be displayed in various forms. Sometimes children misinterpret scolding and rebukes to be a sign of lack of love. It is important to assure the child that he is always loved, even when his behavior warrants disciplinary measures. Such a child becomes confident and happy and will never seek solace elsewhere. The love of the mother becomes a source of happiness and peace at home.

2. Sacrifice and dedication

A mother gives up a great deal for the sake of the child. She gives up her time, her sleep, her pleasures, and many to mention, to ensure that the child is all right. A good mother places the needs of the child, both physical and emotional needs, first and above all. This is an important point to keep in mind, especially in these modern times. Women today are deluded by society into making their own careers and jobs more important than their homes. The home will always remain a woman's most valuable work and that may require all types of sacrifices. It is not really a sacrifice but is an investment which will reap great dividends.

3. Protection and Security

A mother always tries to safeguard the child from danger and difficulties. However, some mothers tend to be over protective. It is wise for the child to learn to face some problems in life, according to his age and circumstances. A coddled child will be unable to face the realities of the world when he grows up, a world which will not be so considerate of him as his mother.

4. A window of the Child to the World

When a child is born, he is totally unaware of the outside world. The mother plays an important part in introducing him to the world. The outlook that the child will form towards life depends a lot on the mother. His attitude, his views, his perspective on life and its goal, will all be gained from her. Eventually he will mature and perhaps form his own changed views, but the initial years and what he learns in them will always have a lasting impression on his mind. A mother is said to be better than a hundred teachers. Her emotional strengths and weaknesses are an example for the child and will be followed for many years to come even though all of it may not be worthy. People have been reported to be following their mother's ways even when they know the mothers were wrong. It is almost an unconscious reaction, and it takes effort to behave differently. Thus, mothers have an important task of setting forth a good example.

Many mothers think it's too great a burden to be acting near perfect all the time, even in the familiarity of their own homes. However, it is a good training. What mothers will change in themselves for their children will become a habit and will lead to a real change. It is not perfection that is being demanded from mothers, but a willingness to accept the responsibility of modeling good acceptable behavior. Many great people remember their mothers and the role they played in nurturing their greatness. Choose to be that mother!

5. Awareness of Responsibility

Motherhood is a career, and those who take it up must try and excel at it. It is the duty of every mother to look onto better techniques and strategies of parenting. When a mother reads about problems that parents face, she is comforted by the fact that she is not alone. That is very reassuring as often parents assume they are the only ones having difficulties. Also, reading about solutions used by other people, or advice given by psychologists, etc. helps broaden the choice of possible tactics in dealing with children.

6. Setting clear Goal

A mother has to know what she expects from her children and then explain that to them. It is not enough to want good children.

The children must know what exactly is expected from them and what the mother wants them to do.

Sometimes a mother tells the child to lay the table properly. Because it has not been explained to the child what properly means, he does it the way he thinks it's right. The child may consequently be blamed for being sloppy, lazy, and other negative traits for not setting the table right. The frustration and heartache could have been avoided if the child knew exactly what was expected from him, rather than a vague order to lay the table. The same can be applied to all chores, behavior with others, academic achievements etc. The mother must have definite goals of what she wants and make them clear.

7. Encouraging Children according to their potential

Each child comes with his own distinctive potential. Children have abilities that could lead to great achievements. Some show skill and interest in a certain area, while others prefer a different one. Apart from not trying to compare children with one another, a good mother tries to bring out the best in each child. She makes the child develop his skills in whatever area he is good at, as well as remedy the weakness in each child. If one child is very shy, for example, the mother should not demand that he socialize and interact with others the way his siblings do. Some mothers unwittingly put their children through a great deal of embarrassment and humiliation.

The child must be taught to overcome his shyness. The mother could give practical suggestions of what the child could talk about to others. A mother's gentle guidance can remedy many flaws and weaknesses in the character of the child.

OCCUPY YOUR CHILDREN

I must admit that being a daughter of a primary teacher (my mother) has given me an advantage in knowing how to occupy my children. I have learned that if you don't occupy your children, they will occupy you! They will do things that annoy you or annoy each other. Even if you haven't been trained, it's not difficult to find ways in spending and investing time in your children. You can start by drawing for them and telling them the names of things from the time they are babies. Give them safe, non-toxic crayons to scribble and draw until they can move on to color pencils. Don't just pour the bucket of bricks for your children to play with by themselves. Rather, sit with them, build with them, encourage them to be imaginative and creative by being there to help them out when their fingers are stuck or when they can't find the piece that might just fit the hole.

Sitting with your children and occupying them gives you precious bonding time. This is when you discover things about your child, his character and his potential. With this insight, you understand your child, you are better equipped to mold his character, to stretch his mind and harness his talent.

With this strong bonding cemented in their childhood, your children will always turn to you as they get older, you will always be the person to turn to when the bricks won't stick together.

An additional tip is to make learning fun. The worksheet, be it writing letters or doing numbers, drawing, coloring, gluing and sticking. Art and craft are naturally incorporate into the worksheets, so they never felt that it was work or in any way tedious.

Children and Play

Most parents view playing as a waste of time. They would like a child to grow out of the love for playing and get into more serious things like studies, research, or even households' chores. It seems more like a childish behavior that must be tolerated, and the sooner is over the better. However, they forget that play is an important part of growing up and is vital for the physical and emotional development of the child. Play is the first source of learning basic social skills necessary for life. A child loves to play, and it is a form of punishment for the child to be deprived of playtime. This desire to play, anywhere and with anything, is most evident in the early years. It is a sigh of emotional and physical health. A child who does not wish to play should be a source of concern.

Benefits of Play

•*Physical benefits*: A child's body develops through physical play. His senses sharpen, his reactions become refined, and he learns the use of appropriate limbs to achieve his goals. In the beginning years, play helps a child to learn about the world around him as he touches and feels the objects within his reach.

His bones become stronger, vision is sharpened and the limbs become stronger. Running and exercising helps the flow of blood and results in a healthier, happier child. Playtime gives your child the message, "You are worth my time. You are a valuable person". It is well known that children learn through play. It improves a child's behavior by giving him feelings of importance and accomplishment. Instead of viewing playtime as a chore, use it to make an investment in your child's behavior. You may feel that you are "wasting time" stacking blocks when you could be "doing something" instead. Of course, you don't have to play all day long, nor will your child want you to (unless he senses your resistance). What may seem like a meaningless activity to you, means a lot to your baby.

Mental benefits: Play provides answers to the curiosity and restlessness of the child. The imagination of a child is very strong, and play helps to bring it out.

A child can thus imagine that he is a principal and his friends are the students, or that he and his friends are part of a family and they take on the role of adults, one being a dad, the other a mum, and friends they become kids, sometimes uncles and aunties. Such play makes the child creative as he puts himself in another's role.

The child also learns certain forms of behavior through play. He learns about fairness and justice, about sharing and caring. He learns to become alert and watchful.

He becomes lively and enthusiastic. He learns to invent solutions when he is in a fix and how to outwit his rivals in play. All these tactics are of great use later in life.

•*Emotional benefits*: Children often get angry when they do not achieve their desire. When they lose a game, they may sulk, or whine, or even attack the rival/s. In time, and through the help and guidance of others, they will learn to control themselves. This is especially true if the play is supervised or at least watched by an adult. Through play, the child will learn to accept defeat, and not feel jealous of another's victory. It removes the self-centeredness that is very common in children.

•*Social benefits:* A child should be encouraged to play with others. Some children are shy and they hesitate to participate in playing with others. Parents should try and contrive gatherings of friends whom the child knows and will feel comfortable with.

He will thus overcome his shyness. Many social problems can be overcome by playing co-operatively with others. Parents today find it difficult to arrange for their children to play with those whom they know and trust. Stressful lifestyles, distances etc. all do their part in keeping children apart. However, parents should try as much as possible to ensure that their children get occasional chances to play with others. Playing at home with siblings or parents also has similar benefits. Children benefit differently from playing.

For many it is a path to gaining confidence, recognizing one's abilities, and learning about others. Play uplifts the spirit of the child, making him cheerful and lively. It removes sorrow and anger and is a good medicine for an unhappy child.

Types of Play

A young child can play with almost anything. He does not need fancy and expensive toys. Simple inexpensive forms of play could include playing with old utensils, scraps of cloth and paper etc. Parents should be creative and look for things the child could play with, rather than buying the latest in the stores. A child who keeps on getting new toys will soon become dissatisfied. Many children these days are quick to lose interest in a toy. They should be shown creative ways of playing.

Forms of play differ according to age and ability of children. Younger children like to play with water, scrap materials, paper and glue, etc.

They like to build and destroy. As they grow older they begin to play in groups. They like organized games and a chance to show their skills through play. Children may develop interest in a particular sport or hobby. Parents should encourage this if possible, and help their child develop his talent.

Parents and Play

It is a great joy for children when their parents play with them. As the child grows, sport and board games could be a chance for the family together. This binds the family closer. But parents should remember that this play is for the sake of the child, not for themselves. They should not seek to have everything according to what they think is right. A little flexibility is recommended. They should also let the child gain some small victories so that he does not despair whenever he plays with the parents. Playing with children is a good way of getting to know the child and his temperaments. It should not however be turned against him with taunts and scolding.

Companions in Play

Children are very influenced by the friends they play with. Parents should be careful that they do not pick up bad habits and behaviors through their play.

If a change in behavior or speech is noticed, parents should at once ask about whom the child plays with. The child should be explained that such forms of behavior will not be tolerated. Some children pick up rude forms of speech, aggressive behavior and even a disrespectful attitude. It is thus necessary to be careful about the playmates of the child. If necessary, the child should be prevented from association with inappropriate playmates.

Some important points:

1. Too much play is harmful for the child. He must not be allowed to spend all his time in play. Life must be a balance, and work is also essential. From childhood, it is necessary to learn that there is a time for everything. So, a child must learn that he cannot run around and touch everything in someone else's home. He cannot play when he has school work or chores to finish. He cannot spend his entire holidays just playing. He needs to do some useful things at the same time.

2. Children must not be forced to play. Some parents insist that their children play with the board game they have bought for them. Or they demand that since the children are bored, they must play outside. If children do not wish to play it is a form of punishment to be forced to do it. Left by themselves, most children will play occasionally.

3. The environment for play must be child-friendly. If there are too many rules and restrictions, it limits the freedom and independence of a child. Some rules are necessary, but sometimes parents become extremely concerned about things around the house, or about the cleanliness and organization of their home. There must be a place for children where they can play freely, even if it means they may make a mess. They should be taught to clean up after themselves, not stopped from ever making a mess.

4. There should be a variety in playing. Different forms of play such as sports, board games, puzzles, imaginative acting, and others, all help to build a healthy and strong character. It is wrong to emphasize on only one form of play and neglect others. A balanced individual has had the chance of trying out and enjoying various forms of recreations and the skills they build.

Outside influences

Human society today is stooping to lower and lower levels of morality. Although many parents try hard to bring up their children in the right manner, a variety of forces sometimes destroy their efforts. The influences of these outside forces often play havoc with the training given at home. This should not be underestimated and parents must be aware of their negative potential. Once the enemy is realized, it becomes easier to control and decrease its impact.

To be able to face these regularly but remain morally intact, they need the help and guidance of wise parents. Children must be taught how to avoid or minimize mental and emotional pollution. Such guidance will be vital for moral stability all through life as these influences will remain. Technological advances have made it possible for children to have various forms of evil and degrading entertainment. Television, computer, internet, and other sources of media are all part of many children's lives.

Although there are advantages that can be derived from these sources, parents have to be vigilant to ensure that children are not drawn to the violence and corruption lurking in them.

Television, cell phones and other tablets

Much has been said and written about this invention which has become a necessary part of every home. In today's world, children have unprecedented access to media and technology. As most parents will attest, young children are drawn to and perhaps even addicted to television/videos, mobile/cell phones, iPad and other tablets available to them in their homes and from the adults around them. There are some advantages to it. There are some good programs and documentaries that broaden the horizons of a child's life and teach him about the world around him.

However, children who are constantly watching shows begin to think that love, beauty, glamour and fun are the aims of life. Wrong messages are absorbed and learnt by the child. These messages are quite effective because they are passed through the medium of sight. Children are bombarded with images of people seemingly leading fun-filled lives. Their behavior, clothing and lifestyles are sometimes wrong. The world, however, seems to admire such people and children begin to admire them too. They wish to emulate them and follow their way of life. This type of subtle brain washing is very dangerous and can greatly influence the mind of a child.

Another disadvantage of television is the amount and degree of violence on TV shows or programs. It is a known fact that regular viewers of television become immune or desensitized to violence. Scenes of death and gruesome violence create no emotion in them. Some viewers are even tempted to carry out what they watch. Human beings lose their gentleness and humanness when they watch a lot of violence. The result is scary. Scores of young television viewers have no concern over the killings and murders that have become a part of life in many parts of the world.

Often, parents see television as a babysitter. What they do not realize is that the children are coming under the influence of what they see. Their minds and thinking become attuned to the pictures flashing on the screen.

It is much better to have children beside the parent while they are working. A mother who is cooking and getting them to help. Or the children could read or color or do any other activities near to her working mother. It is better to think out ways of keeping children busy while parents are working rather than turning on the television the whole time.

Books

A book is the best teacher for a child, a friend who is never far away in times of boredom and loneliness. Reading the correct type of books can influence the child towards what is good and right in life. Parents should introduce their children to a good library and encourage them to read in their spare time.

A great danger is when children begin reading the wrong type of books. Just as books can be a good influence, they can also be a destructive one. A bad book can spoil the mind of a child, filling it with poisonous ideas and views. Many books for children are filled with violence, fantasy and romance. Comics and other such books may be entertaining but have little or no benefit for the child. Parents should know what their children are reading. It is not enough to encourage children to read and then leave them to choose whatever they wish. Most children will choose junk literature which has little benefit for the mind or for literary development. Children must be guided towards choosing good books. Not necessarily boring or didactic ones, but ones which have value in their stories and language. Many libraries these days have information on good books for various ages.

Friends

Another great influence on the life of children is the friends they associate with. The child's values and self-concept are affected by persons of significance in his life; relatives, coaches, teachers, religious leaders and friends. Keep a watchful eye on your child's friendships. Sometimes, parents may run into the idea that a young child should be exposed to children with different values so that he can choose for himself. This may sound good but it tends not to work. It's like sending a ship to sea without a rudder or a captain. Only by chance will that ship reach a desired destination. Children are too valuable to be left to chance.

Your child's friends are people who are around your child enough to influence her behavior and model values. Once upon a time the persons of significance in a child's life came primarily from within the extended family, but in today's mobile society a child is likely to have a wider variety of peers and persons of significance. This means that today's parents need to be vigilant as to who is modeling what behavior to their children. Here is where there is confusion in the ranks of parents as disciplinarians. There are two extremes. On the one side are the parents who feel it's healthy for children to experience a lot of different value systems while growing up so that they will be more open-minded as adults. On the other side are parents who want to protect their child from all outside influences and any ideas that may differ from their own beliefs. This child grows up in a bubble-like atmosphere. Somewhere between these two extremes is the right answer to raise a confident child.

Throwing a child into the melting pot of diverse values at a very young age before she has any of her own values may produce a child who is so confused that she/he develops no conscience and no standing value system Parents who overprotect may end up with a child who cannot think for herself/himself, leaving her/him vulnerable to challenges or so judgmental that she/he condemns anyone with different beliefs. Somewhere in the middle is the parent who grounds the child in a firm value system and guides her/him as she/he encounters other value systems. The child because she/he has a strong value system to begin with, is better able to weigh her/his parents 'value system against alternatives and develop one's own firm code of values. It may be different from the parents'. It may include many of the parents' values with a sprinkling of alternatives learned from peers or teachers. But the important thing is that the child has a value system from which to operate.

Middle childhood, is the age from which your children build consciences and learn your value system. In fact, it's the only time in their entire life when they unquestionably, at least early in that stage, accept their parents' value system.

Slowly they form their own standards through neighborhood relationships schools and church/synagogue friendships. They discover a larger world with a variety of beliefs and behaviors. As they talk (endlessly) and observe experiment in a variety of situations, they learn about how they will choose to act and react.

Coupling a passive person with a strong personality is all right if the stronger child pulls your child up rather than knocking him/her down. Let your child choose his/her own friends and monitor the relationships. At the end of a play examine your child's feelings. While some children will wisely seek out complimentary playmates on their own, sometimes it is helpful to set up your child by purposely exposing him to appropriate peers. Some groups of children just naturally seem to get along well. Many people stray from the straight path as a result of the negative influence of friends. There is no doubt that the behavior of a friend can affect a child. He/she picks up mannerisms, ways of speech and other expressions from the friends he/she plays with and works with all day. Especially when children are at school, the hours spent with classmates often have great influence. A child is often naïve, and believes what others tell him/her, especially the peers. A child without control may have the wrong friends, get involved in the wrong activities and generally begin to have very different morals and values from them.

You can invite home your child's friends. Yes, you will have messes to clean up, but it's worth it. Hosting the neighborhood helps you monitor your child; it gives you the opportunity to observe your child's social style and generally learn more about your child's personality, which social behaviors are appropriate and which need improving. When children are well equipped to manage different environments (home, grandparents, preschool, ballet class, etc.) with different rules very well according to each place, it's a great package for a lifetime.

Although it is necessary for children to spend time with their friends, parents should discourage going out all the time with friends, especially as the children get older. By being aware of the influences that effect the child, parents can try and combat them. They can minimize their effects by keeping the child away from them as much as possible. Good friends can make a great difference to the molding of character. Thus, a parent has to be vigilant of the child's friends. Always being in the company of one who has "loose morals" or a dirty tongue, or other such vices, will rub off on the child. Discourage very close connections such as frequent telephone calls, sleeping over at each other's homes and any other affinities. Moderation in all fields is necessary for progress. It is necessary for a child to have friends but it is also necessary that the parents know whom the child befriends.

Although it is not possible to protect the child totally from all negative influences, nor is it wise to cocoon him completely, it is important that a young child be protected as much as possible. As they become older they become more and more exposed to such influences. But then the child is mature enough to hold on to his or her own beliefs and values, and the damage is much less.

Sibling's Rivalry

Whenever there are two or more children in a family, rivalry between them is inevitable. Jealousy is a very common trait in human beings. People look at the successes of others and react in one of the two ways. Some wish to achieve the same and thus try to work for it. Harboring no ill-feelings or grudge. Others however, wish to despoil the good fortune they see.

Their nature is such that they cannot bear to see the success of others, and hope for its destruction. It is not abnormal for children to feel jealous of one another. The aim of parents should be to control it and keep it within appropriate limits. It cannot be totally eliminated. When confronted with the achievement of a sibling, many children perceive it as a threat. They are afraid of losing their status. Success of a sibling could result in unfavorable comparisons, greater expectations and lower respect for themselves, both at home and outside. Although this could be entirely imaginary and blown out of protection, it is necessary to understand why children react as they do. Most siblings' rivalry stems from the perceived loss of parental love and respect. Children wish to have the greatest share of their parents love and attention. When siblings take it away from them, even temporarily, it becomes greatly upsetting. Only time and maturity help the child understand that this loss is only imagined and not real.

An important point to consider is that it is sometimes possible for a parent to love one child more than another. It could be because of certain qualities the child possesses. The parent has to be very careful, however, not to display this inclination. It could result in great jealousy.

Causes of Jealousy

•**Position in danger:** When a new baby is born in the family, the child who was the youngest (or the only one) feels threatened. He is accustomed to being the center of attention and now has to contend with someone who takes away the parent's love and attention. This is especially true of younger children who cannot understand that the parents have enough love for all their children. The demands of a newborn are often misunderstood. In such a situation the feeling of sibling rivalry can be reduced through the following ways:

a. Talk to the child before the baby arrives. Prepare him and involve him in the preparations for the new arrival. It could become a very exciting event if handled properly. The child will begin to feel attached to the baby before it comes and will await the arrival anxiously.

b. When the baby arrives, involve the child as much as possible. He could carry out small chores according to her age, such as bringing diapers, holding the towel, etc. The feeling of being a big sister or brother creates a sense of importance and makes the loss of position more bearable. The child is now evolving towards a higher status and must be taught to appreciate that.

c. Talk to the child constantly. Discuss the baby with the sibling/s. Talk about his walking up at night, his crying, his babyish gestures and the like. Keeping communication open with the children assures them of the love of the parents.

Comparing

All human beings (including children) have different abilities and personalities. A variety of characters and traits in a family make the home a lively and interesting place. Many parents however, make the mistake of constantly comparing children with one another. Although the intent is to try and make one child imitate the good behavior of another, the result is often resentment and jealousy.

If you want to raise a confident child, be sure your child believes you value her because of who she is, not how she performs. Do this by giving her plenty of eye contact, touching and focused attention. Don't expect your child to excel in sports or music or academics just because you did. The one thing your child can excel in is being herself. She must know that your love for her does not depend on your approval of her performance. That's a tough assignment for a parent who may have been raised to perform for love and acceptance.

Comparison lowers the self-esteem of children, especially when one child is always at a disadvantage. Sometimes children are given labels, so one may be "lazy" another 'smart", another "slow" and other epithets. Such labels or tagging, especially if given constantly, eventually become accepted and believed. A "slow" child comes to believe that he is slow and may never wholly overcome it.

At times parents compare their children to those of other families. It is all right to sometimes mention the good qualities of another child, but it must be done gently and carefully. It is wrong to praise other children and lower one's own, especially if this is done constantly. Every child searches for an identity and, when found, clings to it like a trademark.

•**Giving more attention to one child:** Sometimes a child needs more attention than others. This could be true of small babies, or if a child is sick and/or has a particular problem. When a parent gives continuous attention to one child, it is natural that the others feel resentful and jealous. The first thing to do is ascertain

that the child receiving more attention actually needs it. Some children just demand more.

If it is a genuine need, it must be explained to the other children. Just discussing it with them and talking about why more attention is given to the sibling may help in preventing anger and jealousy. It is also necessary to find some time spend alone with each child. This is hard to do when parents are very busy, but an effort must be made. A small amount of time spent alone with one child could make a great difference in bolstering his confidence and security.

Hints for reducing Sibling's Rivalry

1. Deal with justice. Justice does not mean the same treatment for everyone. It has been defined by as placing a thing in its space. Differences in treatment to children will exist because of age differences. A five-year old and a teenager will not have the same bedtime. Nor will both of them receive the same type of clothing or toys. Justice means to treat each child with appropriate respect and consideration.

When differences are present, explain to the child the reasons and assure them that they too will receive the same treatment when appropriate.

2. If a child displays jealousy toward another sibling, parents should not become shocked and try to suppress it. No parent can force a child to love his sibling or threaten him if he shows signs of jealousy. If that is done, the child may learn only that he should not display his jealousy in front of the parent. He may carry the feeling with him for a long time. Today there are many adults who hold grudges against their siblings. To avoid that, parents should try and deal with it in the initial stages. Patience and understanding are required, especially for the very young one who sometimes show even violent signs of jealousy.

Although conflict and constant bickering is very common in children, most people grow out of it. Many siblings grow up to be very close to each other even if they may be physically miles apart. Siblings rivalry is a source of great concern to many parents, and many wonder in frustration if their children will ever get along with one another. However, this can be overcome with some wisdom and tact and a lot of patience. Eventually the bond between siblings becomes, for most people, stronger than many bonds.

MISTAKES PARENTS OFTEN MAKE

Many parents have frustrated and angry relationships with their children. Even if very young children sometimes become a source of annoyance with their constant demands, whining and disobedience, family life is supposed to be joyous and fulfilling.

If parents would take a little time and effort to improve their ways, realize their mistakes, and devise new strategies and plans, the dividends would be great. A small change in attitude and/or behavior would make life much happier for both parent and child. Below are some common mistakes that parents often make:

1. Making children dependent: Some parents believe that to love children means to do their work. They take excessive pity on the child and feel that as parents it is their duty to do things for him. So, at six years old a child is still being dressed by the parents. He is considered too young to tie his own shoes or comb his hair. Such constant fussing over the child does not instill confidence and independence in the child. A ten-year-old child who never cleans his room, and lets mom or dad do it, will learn to always depend on others. This may also foster laziness, sloppiness and a lack of initiative. A wise parent knows that the best way to help a child is not doing things for him, but to show him how to do them. Learning the skills of carrying out personal and household chores are an achievement often appreciated during the early years. A Child who is not taught to do them when young, will be very unwilling to do them when she/he gets older. Parents should help their children learn to do their own work. Spoiling a child creates weakness and a lack of will and determination. These types of children trouble their parents in their childhood and make them encounter many problems.

The spoilt children themselves face two types of problems:

a. They have expectations that the rest of society will, like their parents, comfort and respect them no matter what, and carry out their wishes without any question. When they realize that people will not only refuse to do this, but will also ridicule these expectations, they become upset and feel humiliated and debased.

b. Such experiences form the base of contempt and make them angry, aggressive lacking patience and weak. They become the type of people who think low of others and treat them with harsh words and actions. Nothing silences the sense of self-trust in a child more than forcing him to do things they may not have the capability of doing. This is especially the case when, if the child is unsuccessful, it is followed by belittling of statements like: "Don't bother trying, you can't, you don't have the capability."

2. Quarreling in front of the children: It is natural for couples to have occasional arguments, sometimes even heated and bitter ones. However, it is very damaging to carry these out in front of children. Children do not understand that this is not a cause of worry and may begin to imagine the worst. To them it could be a sign that the parents do not love each other, that they may even divorce and destroy his world. This causes depression and loss of security among children. Worse, it could have damaging effects as the child grows. He could look upon the conflicting relationship of his parents as a normal relationship for married couples and this could have a major effect on his own relationships. Some parents even try to make the children take sides. If a wife feels her husband is treating her unfairly, she may talk to the children and make them see her side. She would like to turn them against the husband, at least to a certain degree. What she fails to realize is that the husband is a father to her children. They would like to respect and love him.

By poisoning them against him, she is doing them a great injustice. She could be damaging a relationship that has the potential to bring the child great good. This also applies to those who try to turn children against their grandparents, or their relatives.

Because of a conflict with in-laws, children are told of how unfair and oppressive the family is.

To deprive the children of love and respect for their extended family is also a great wrong. Parents should not let their own quarrels keep their children away from enjoying the special love of grandparents and other relatives.

The best thing parents can do to a child is present a loving and harmonious relationship among themselves. It boosts the child both mentally and emotionally and helps him form loving relationships in his own life. It is true that arguments cannot always be dismissed. But they must be done in private, away from the child who cannot understand or bear fighting among his parents.

3. Expecting too much of children: In normal development, a child moves out from the known into the unknown. She tries out new experiences in much the same way that an attached infant learns to separate from mother. It is quite normal for a child to retreat periodically into the comfort of the known (her home and family) as she progressively ventures into the jungle of the unknown. It is important for the child to have a strong attachment base. Being shy does not mean that a child has a poor self-image. She needs an extra dose of confidence so that she can follow her own inner timetable in adjusting to new situations and relationships.

If you see no change in the child's willingness to venture out, that may be unhealthy.

But if you see some gradual moving out, then your child is simply a cautious social developer. Some parents would like their children to behave totally like adults. They don't want them to run around, to play, to talk loudly, even to touch things around the house. What they should understand is that all these activities are part of growing up. To be a healthy adult, children need to have passed through various stages, each of which is a building block in his character.

The child lives in a world quite different from that of the parent. Parents sometimes view the life of the child from an adult perspective and forget that to the child his little world is very important. Although they must be kept away from harmful and dangerous things, a child should be allowed to explore things that arouse his curiosity. Let him meddle with things that he is interested in, if the consequences are not very destructive. The house should not be a prison for him, with constant orders to sit down and be quiet.

Allow the child to have a little independence, especially in things that are not greatly significant. The small mistakes that he may make will teach him to do different next time. There is a difference between issues of grave importance that cannot be compromised, and issues in which some flexibility can be allowed. Life should not be so serious that every small thing should be treated like a major issue. Some parents also make the mistake of expecting too many achievements from their children. A parent should know his child. And his strengths and weaknesses. If a child is not too bright, it is enough to encourage him to work hard and achieve according to his potential. To expect that he must bring perfect marks and then show disappointment when he cannot, hurts the child and lowers his self-esteem. This is the same for all expectations the parents have from the child. It must be proportionate to the age and ability of their child.

4. Negativity: Life is miserable for those children who have to deal with parents who are constantly negative. Such parents do not forget mistakes, harp on small issues, and are always predicting the worst. "You are not studying hard; you are bound to fail." "Your room is such a mess, I wonder how sloppy your house will be when you grow up", "stop troubling your younger sister, you have no love for her at all" are examples of negative and perhaps destructive comments.

A parent may sometimes say such things in anger, but it is the constant repetition of negative comments that affect a child greatly. A happy home is one in which children know that they will be disciplined when necessary, but do not have to fear a sharp tongue or harsh words. Some parents also have a very negative attitude on life. They complain of their work and the people they work with. They blame the world for their troubles and are quick to talk negatively about others.

All this is undoubtedly going to have an effect on the child. A child who has heard a lot about how unfair and difficult life is may form a dim view of life in this world. His enthusiasm for life decreases. A great deal of a child's joy and zest for living stems from what parents think and say about life. It is always necessary to avoid being too negative when talking in front of children.

5. Being two-faced: Many parents do not realize how observant and absorbing a child is. They will talk in front of him forgetting that he is present, almost as though he is a piece of furniture, deaf and dumb. But a child listens and absorbs, often ponders over and sometimes repeats what he hears. Thus, when a parent says something about a particular thing or person, and then says something different to someone else, the child is introduced to being two-faced.

A parent may rant against someone and say he dislikes him immensely. Yet when he meets the same person, he is very nice to him and shows no sign of his anger. Although to a certain degree this may be necessary, for we cannot show our disagreements openly, it is not necessary to indulge in hypocritical behavior. A hypocrite is one who will be very sweet to the face but will stab from the back. A child should not be exposed to such behavior. He believes that his parent is always right and to see such two-faced behaviors is a disillusionment and wrong message.

6. Humiliating a child in front of others: A child has his own personality and just like an adult, wants that others should love and respect him. It is thus very difficult for him when he is scolded and derogated in public. Some parents announce to others when the children are present, how well behaved one child is and how naughty the other. Or, if a mistake is made, he is scolded even when there are other people around. A slight reprimand may not matter too much, but a serious one should be done in private. Respect the child's personality and you will teach him to respect others.

Parents are human and bound to make mistakes. The aim is not to refrain from ever making mistakes but to learn from them and gradually decrease them. Parents have been making the same mistakes over the years, and it is time to learn and change. A slight change in attitude and methods of parenting will create vastly improved relationships between parents and children.

RELATIONSHIPS & CHILDREN

To guide them properly, we must show natural affection to children from the very beginning as this will help the natural flow later on as they develop. As mentioned previously, Infants need to be physically, socially, and emotionally cared for. Keep them clean and fed, let them play with other kids once in a while as this helps develop their social skills at a very young age, and meet all of their needs kindly and consistently but avoid spoiling them with gifts. From this steady, predictable care, infants develop a sense of emotional security and learn that they can trust other people. Constantly give approval to them. Watch, applaud, hug, and kiss them when they lift their heads, turn over, crawl, sit up. Encourage them when stammering their first words or when attempting to stand.

Be kind and patient as infants learn to do things for themselves. Harsh correction could diminish the ability and fear of trying new things, lower their self-esteem and make them anxious about trusting others. For instance, if a little girl tries to feed herself and constantly spills her food and her father habitually becomes angry, she may come to believe that she is bad because she spills. Encouraging her to try again in a calm and loving voice would make her want to do more and eventually, she will get good at it. She may also learn to fear men as she may think they are harsh and loud if you always react angrily. Her father's challenge is to find a clean spot on which to kiss her and to encourage her to keep trying day after day, at her own pace, until she develops the needed skill. Through all stages of growth, children need parental encouragement.

Punishment for failure will make them feel inferior and unwilling to develop close relationships. Pressure to progress faster than they are ready can create emotional frustration, a feeling of not being good enough, and for no matter how much they are forced, they cannot do more than their young motor skills and immature coordination will allow. A baby must learn by trial and error how to maneuver the spoon from bowl to mouth. Food will spill until the time when, after much practice, his or her brain gains control and balance as the cerebrum develops and coordinates with his or her eyes, arms, and mouth muscles, perfecting the movement of the spoon from bowl to mouth.

Be loving when you correct your children as this will determine whether they will be willing to try again next time. Do not withhold affection from them as a way to chastise them, for they may not learn to give affection to others.

Physical or emotional abuse may teach a child that cruelty is the normal way to treat other people that might cause violence in a long run as they get older. Also, avoid making a child fearful by locking him in a dark room or threatening to leave him alone as this might have an emotional effect on the child and they might make it their comfort zone and not deal with problems later on in life, but instead, go hide in a dark room, hide and push people they care about away.

The first contribution of the home to the happiness of the child is to impress him with the fact that there are bounds beyond which he cannot go with safety. Second, to teach and show him to be considerate of the rights of others. Third, to have him feel that home is a place where confidences and consolations are exchanged. And fourth, to have him cherish the thought that home is a place of seclusion and rest from the worries and perplexities of life because no matter what life throws at you, there will always be a place to return to, and let them know home is the first and main attempt if anything goes wrong or right.

WAYS TO IMPROVE A YOUNG CHILD'S BEHAVIOUR

•*Discipline*: This is different for each stage of your child's development. For younger children, keep the discipline simple and easy to understand. These little ones do not yet have the language skills or reasoning abilities that an older child or an adult has.

•*Consistency*: Be consistent, it's an effective discipline tool. Children of every age are smart and very adept at sensing indecision or wavering in parents. Being a consistent disciplinarian can be overwhelming, particularly with young children. But the truth is you are the parent and you are in charge. By being consistent, the child begins to know what to expect and feels secure within the rules of the house. Consistency equals calmness in a household.

•*Give a chance to make choices:* Children, like any other person, like to be given a room to make their choices. It's important to give them some freedom of choice. Won't it be so boring if someone has to tell you what you have to eat and wear every day, and who you would socialize with each and every day?

Each day is a loving form of discipline that is likely to decrease their tantrums and acting out. The point here is to help your child avoid feeling so powerless on a daily basis that he reacts by acting out in inappropriate ways. Naturally, this won't always work and your child may simply tell you, "I don't want to do this or that." That's when you will let your child know that if he can't, then you will choose for him.

•*Listen to the Child's wishes:* Sometimes a child is opposed to what the parent wishes him to do. This could be as simple as an enforcement of bedtime, wearing of appropriate clothes, or going for a particular outing, etc. The child may have a different view as to what should be done. A good parent would listen to what the child has to say. This does not mean that the parent gives in to the child or lets him do as he wishes, it just means that the parent respects the child's opinions, although not necessarily following it. The child will eventually do as the parent wishes but will feel that he was listened to.

•*Give consequences and rewards.* It's good when there are always consequences for your child's actions, both positive and negative. Throughout life, we all have to live with the consequences of our actions. If you don't go to work on time each day, it is likely you will be fired.

One of the most important tools a parent can teach their children is that when they behave in a certain way, there will be certain consequences that follow. Giving consequences and sticking to them is important. Your child should know that if he breaks the rules, there will be a consequence for that choice. No one in the family should get away with changing the rules to fit their own needs and feelings. Children are able to understand that if you have a consequence that is not to their liking, their behavior will change quickly, so that they are able to join back in the fun. They are smart enough to grasp the concept that naughty behavior equals serious consequences and will generally adapt to whatever expectations you have for them. When your child succeeds at something, give her a big treat. It's also helpful to ask your child what he would like to work towards earning; that way, you will also know what motivates him.

There are some typical statements that parents of any age can be heard making: *"Kids of nowadays are so ungrateful...", "In our time, we were much more disciplined and obedient...", "We never shouted at our parents the way kids answer us back nowadays.* I have hardly ever come across a parent who openly admits to having made a parenting mistake, e.g. saying something like: "I should have not scolded my daughter in front of her friends. I think she deserves an apology." More often, we find parents acting holier and judgmental in front of their children, discussing their children's weaknesses before friends and relatives, and detailing how difficult their children can make life for them.

However, how often do we come across a parent who would readily apologize to their children for mistreating them? Or admit to being wrong in front of them? On the contrary, parents hardly ever publicly admit to making mistakes in their children's upbringing.

Be a strong Moral Example

Parents are their children's first and most powerful moral teachers, so make sure the moral behaviors your kids are picking up from you are the ones that you want them to copy. Try to make your life a living example of good moral behavior for your child to see. Each day ask yourself: "If my child had only my behavior to watch, what example would he/she catch?" The answer is often quite telling.

As parents, you are the best example the children can have. If you talk to your parents rudely, expect your children to do the same to you. If you are disrespectful to others, don't get surprised if your children follow too.

No one can put on a happy face all the time, but a parent's unhappiness can transfer to a child. Your child looks to you as a mirror for his own feelings. If you are worried, you can't reflect good feelings. Just be realistic. You can't be up and smiling all the time and still be human. Your child should know that parents have down days, too.

Children can see through fake cheerfulness. Your sensitivity toward him will increase his sensitivity toward you, and someday he may be the one lifting your self-confidence. Try to be positive as much as you can. The world already has its bad side waiting to be revealed to your kid, and he may be influenced, so let him enjoy the good side of it at home at least, by your side.

As mentioned earlier, children are easily influenced by their surroundings. With television, radio, internet, and forms of media mostly touting unhuman values. It is up to parents and adults close to the children to set the correct example.

It is impossible to shield our children from all the negative forces that can shape their minds and, ultimately, their behavior. However, by our own example and showing them better options, we can set them on the true path, which is to obey. Kindness begets kindness. If we were kind to our children, they, in turn, would show kindness to others.

There is a story I heard that really touched me: Once there lived a traveler. Seeing him sowing seeds in every place he visits, someone asked: "Why are you planting trees through the places which you would never come back to?"

"Well, I may not come back to here," he replied. "It is just because you don't travel around, you live with the fallacy that all the trees we plant are for ourselves.

All these trees and flowers we pass through by relishing and delighting are not grown by us, are they? Aren't we adoring the trees fostered by others? Hence, for this world and nature around strew at least a flower seed."

I remember back home when I was still a kid, my siblings and I would enjoy the mangoes of a tree in our garden, planted by our mum's friend. She moved to a far country and never tasted any of them, but I have never eaten any other mango as testy as those back home. There is also that story of a poor boy, who lived in a city of America. Electricity was not invented then. At nights, the boy was witnessing many pedestrians falling in trouble, due to the trenches and cavities in the road. He decided to help them and lighted up an oil lamp in front of his home. So, it was dark everywhere except his small hut. Passengers praised him and slowly his neighbors began to emulate him. Eventually, the streets of that small town gleamed with small lights and oil lamps, even after the sun sets down on the horizon. The city is Philadelphia, the word means *'brotherly love'*.

While we strew a seed or plant a tree, the goodness reaches to numerous living beings! So, imagine planting the right seed in your children, thinking about those they will meet, thinking about how the world may be a better place, at least their world!

Know your Beliefs and Share them

Before you can raise a moral child, you must be clear about what you believe in. Take time to think through your values then share them regularly with your child, explaining why you feel the way you do. After all, your child will be hearing endless messages that counter your beliefs, so it's essential that he/she hears about your moral standards. It's important to make them understand why they have to do what we, as parents, make them do.

One of the simplest ways to help kids learn new behaviors is to reinforce them as they happen. So, purposely catch your child acting morally and acknowledge his or her good behavior by describing what he or she did right and why you appreciate it.

Studies argue that children who act morally have parents who expect them to do so. Post your moral standards at home then consistently reinforce them until your child internalizes them so they become his or her rules too. It will set a standard for your child's conduct and also will let her know in no uncertain terms what you value.

Encourage your child to lend a hand to make a difference in his world, and always help him or her recognize the positive effect the gesture had on the recipient. The real goal is for kids to become less and less dependent on adult guidance by incorporating moral principles into their daily lives and making them their own.

That can happen only if parents emphasize the importance of the virtues over and over and their kids repeatedly practice those moral behaviors.

Reflect on the behaviors' effects

Researchers tell us that one of the best moral-building practices is to point out the impact of the child's behavior on the other person. Doing so enhances a child's moral growth: ("See, you made her cry.") or highlight the victim's feeling ("Now he feels bad."). The trick is to help the child really imagine what it would be like to be in the victim's place, so he or she will be more sensitive to how his or her behavior impacts others. Research finds that parents who feel strongly about their kids turning out morally usually succeed because they committed themselves to that effort. If you really want to raise a moral child, then make a personal commitment to raise one.

Be Consistent in Your Behavior

Consistent discipline is the cornerstone of every child's wellbeing and will follow them throughout their development and into their adult lives. Consistency is more valuable than extreme behavior of any kind. Our children will be more likely to believe our teachings and follow our examples if we strive to be consistent. One father reacted angrily to his daughter's failing grades in school. His worry about her future overcame his resolve to reason with her. They exchanged harsh words and parted with painful feelings. After calming down, this father went to his daughter and, embracing her, said that he loved her and that his emotions were caused by concern, not dislike. They shed tears, and the bond between them was strengthened. Over the next several months, the father consistently expressed his love for his daughter, and she improved in her schoolwork until she became an excellent student. This father was not yet perfect in setting an example, but he was consistent in expressing love.

SELF-ESTEEM AND CHILDREN

Self-esteem is defined as feeling oneself worthy of the respect of others. Self-esteem is similar to self-worth (how much a person values himself). This can change from day to day or from year to year, but overall, self-esteem tends to develop from infancy and keep going until we are adults. All human beings have an innate desire to be respected and liked. They want others to look up to them. There is great wealth in self-esteem. It brings confidence in one's own abilities and helps in initiating and achieving one's goals. Feeling good about oneself brings peace and happiness to the heart. It boosts the spirit and produces noble characters and lofty ideas.

Self-esteem also can be defined as feeling capable while also feeling loved. A child who is happy with an achievement but does not feel loved may eventually experience low self-esteem. Likewise, a child who feels loved but is hesitant about his or her own abilities can also develop low self-esteem. Healthy self-esteem comes when a good balance is maintained. It's wise to think about developing and promoting self-esteem during childhood.

As kids try, fail, try again, fail again, and then finally succeed, they develop ideas about their own capabilities. At the same time, they are creating a self-concept based on interactions with other people. This is why parental involvement is a key to helping kids form accurate, healthy self-perceptions. Healthy self-esteem is like a child's armor against the challenges of the world. Kids who know their strengths and weaknesses and feel good about themselves seem to have an easier time handling conflicts and resisting negative pressures. In contrast, kids with low-esteem can find challenges to be sources of major anxiety and frustration. Those who think poorly of themselves have a hard time finding solutions to problems. If given to self-critical thoughts such as: "I'm not good" or "I can't do anything right," they may become passive, withdrawn, or depressed. Faced with a new challenge, their immediate response might be 'I can't."

Self-esteem is your child's passport to a lifetime of mental health and social happiness. It's the foundation of a child's well-being and the key to success as an adult. Kids with low self-esteem may not want to try new things and may speak negatively about themselves: "I'm stupid," "I will never learn how to do this," or "What is the point? Nobody cares about me anyway." They may exhibit a low tolerance for frustration, giving up easily, or waiting for somebody else to take over. They tend to be overly critical of and easily disappointed in themselves. Kids with healthy self-esteem tend to enjoy interacting with others. They are comfortable in social settings and enjoy group activities as well as independent pursuits. When challenges arise, they can work toward finding solutions and voice discontent without belittling themselves or others. For example, rather than saying, "I'm an idiot," a child with healthy self-esteem says, "I don't understand this." They know their strengths and weaknesses and accept them. A sense of optimism prevails. At all ages, how you feel about yourself affects how you act. Think about a time when you were feeling really good about yourself. You probably found it much easier to get along with others and feel good about them.

Self-esteem is different from vanity. When a person has some good qualities and/or abilities, to know that and be thankful for it is self-esteem. To be proud about it and to think oneself to be better than others is vanity. From a very young age, children show a desire for respect and attention. They show off in order to get praise. Sometimes when attention is not forthcoming, they revert to negative behavior such as fighting and screaming in order to get attention. There are various views on the origins of this desire for respect.

Some psychologists believe it stems a natural desire for success over others. Others say it comes from a love of self, an egoism inherent in all human beings.

Advantage of a Healthy Self-Esteem

Healthy self-esteem doesn't mean being narcissistic or arrogant. If you raise a confident child that grows up with a healthy self-worth, it means they have a realistic understanding of their strengths and weaknesses, enjoying the strengths, and working on the problem areas. Because there is such a strong parallel between how your child feels about himself and how he acts, it is vital to discipline to raise a confident child.

Below are some advantages of a Child with a healthy Self-Esteem:

1. The child who knows that he has some good qualities that others respect is satisfied with himself. This will translate into rational and calm behavior. There will be no need for tantrums and aggressiveness to demand attention. A child with self-esteem is a happy child.

2. Such a child values himself and knows that he has certain respect and dignity. Thus, there will be lesser chances for him to become involved in acts which lower envisions for himself. A child who respects himself will not easily give in to peer pressure to perform immoral and indecent acts. He would realize that it is beneath himself to stoop to it.

3. A child with a *healthy* self-esteem will try harder to achieve high goals. He knows he is capable of good and can set lofty targets to achieve. He will have the initiative to start things and get involved in

various activities.

When self-esteem is lacking:

1. The child gives in to wrong more easily. He is easily swayed by others as it is difficult to be firm on one's own principles when there is no confidence in oneself. The views and opinions of others will carry great weight. Such children run a higher risk of succumbing to peer pressure and joining unseemly groups.

2. A child who has no self-esteem accepts failure as his lot. He will not try to challenge himself or have high expectations of himself. He does not think he has the ability to achieve anything good. This resignation to failure sets ground for future defeats and the lack of struggle to progress in life.

3. He suffers more from negative emotions such as anger, jealousy, frustration, etc. A child who has confidence in himself can accept another child's success as he knows that he too is successful. But when that consolation is absent, jealousy is a natural reaction. Often there is anger at oneself, or even at others, who may be seen as responsible for the failures. There is then little room for happy, healthy feelings necessary to make the child an emotionally stable human being.

How to foster Self-Esteem in a Child

When you raise a confident child, you spend the early years building your child's self-confidence, and you spend the later years protecting it. Helping your child develop talents and acquire skills is part of discipline. She can do well at something, whether as a two-year-old who packs exceptional pretend picnics or a ten-year-old who loves ballet. If you recognize an ability in your child, encourage him. Strike a balance between pushing and protecting, both are necessary. If you don't encourage your child to try, his skills don't improve, and you have lost a valuable confidence builder. If you don't protect your child from unrealistic expectations, his sense of competence is threatened.

Parents may misunderstand the meaning of self-esteem and feel that this is just one more thing they are required to give their child along with regular meals. They guard against anything that may undercut self-esteem, to the point where it becomes ridiculous. They measure self-esteem daily, as one might take a temperature. ("Brill's self-esteem is low today. Her sister beat her last night.")

Every infant whose needs are met in most cases has self-esteem built in. Like an arborist caring for a tree, in order to raise a confident child, your job is to nurture what's there, do what you can to structure your child's environment so that she grows strong and straight, and avoid whiting away at the tender branches.

You don't need a degree in psychology to raise a confident child. Much of parenting is fun. Hold your baby, respond sensitively to her needs, enjoy your baby. Then sit back and enjoy the person whose self-esteem is developing naturally.

Many parents do not feel it necessary to respect the child. They expect respect but believe that respecting the child will spoil him/her.

However, respect for the child in the following ways will help the child feel good about himself, as well as respect the parent more willingly:

•Talk to the child in a normal voice. Don't belittle the child by talking in a childish voice. Talk to him constantly, not only when you want to scold him or tell him to do something. Talk about everyday affairs; school, work, political issues, stories from your past, etc. Some parents believe that because children do not understand at the level of adults, there is not much use in talking to them. But children who are talked to more often become more understanding and insightful than those who are not.

These children feel a sense of communication with the parents and know that their parents deem them worthy of a conversation. It is a great boost in confidence.

• When scolding the child, do not totally destroy his feeling of self-worth.

Reprove him for a particular action rather than a general "you are good for nothing" attitude, which, if dealt out constantly, will lead the child to actually believe it. As quick as parents are to point out a wrong act, they should remember there are good qualities also present in the child.

• Listen to his ideas and opinions. When the child wishes to say what he thinks of something, encourage him to talk. Don't ridicule or put him down. A child will not have a wisdom of an adult but deserves to be listened to so that he will be forthcoming in his views in future. Dismissing a child's opinions as unworthy is a perfect way to suppress any thoughtfulness or creativity in the child. Sometimes, speak positively about your child to others. When a child hears himself being talked about positively, he feels that it is a sincere appreciation. Long or undeserved praises are not needed, but when the child does something good, mention it to a relative, or a friend, etc. This will seem more genuine and have more effect than a word of praise to the child himself. Parents who criticize and complain about the child to others, in front of the child, often ruin any feeling of self-worth the child may have. As previously mentioned, sometimes parents and relatives act as if the child cannot hear. They discuss about the child in his presence, complaining about what he did to others and mentioning the bad qualities he has.

This has a very negative effect on the child. Parents should be careful with what they say. Kids can be sensitive to parents' and other's words.

Remember to praise your child not only for a job well done but also for effort and be truthful. For example, if your child doesn't make the soccer team, avoid saying something like, "Well, next time you will work harder and make it." Instead, try, "Well, you didn't make the team but I'm really proud of the effort you put into it." Reward effort and completion instead of outcome.

Particular Do's and Don'ts for fostering self-esteem

Do give your child responsibility at home. Give him basic duties and chores, according to his age. It is important that the child feels he is part of the household and is needed for the daily work that goes into running the home.

Do talk to him about major changes or decisions being made for the family. If a new house is being bought, or a job is being changed, let the child know about it. Often, parents leave the child completely out of important decisions being made.

Do teach him not to accept undue or flattery. The child likes to be praised but should only accept it when deserved.

Don't interfere with everything your child does. The child needs some space for healthy independence and originality.

If he wishes to arrange his things in a particular way, for example, or plans something for himself, let him do it as long as it is not wrong in any serious way. Some parents expect that children will do everything exactly as they wish and fuss over every small detail in the child's life. Such a child grows up to feel he cannot make any decision for himself.

Don't pamper the child too much when he is sick or hurt. The child should be taught to be strong and bear a little pain. If allowed to whine and cry a great deal, the child may learn to be a complainer and will be unable to bear difficulties.

Don't ignore the child when you have company. When a family has guests, it's true that the host should pay great respect to the guests. Although this does not mean the children should be ignored and brushed aside. Instead, the parent should encourage the child to be part of the gathering and involve him with the guests.

ENCOURAGE CHILDREN TO EXPRESS THEIR FEELINGS

Raise a confident child by teaching them to express their feelings comfortably. Expressing feelings comfortably does not mean the child is free to explode at every emotional twinge, but rather develops a comfortable balance between expressing and controlling feelings. She should eventually be able to keep a lid on her emotions when needed, but not so tightly that she can't remove the lid in a "safe" setting, such as exercising (i.e., run like mad to blow off steam), or with a trustworthy friend.

Too much control or too much emotion will both produce problems in adult life. Stuffing feelings doesn't do any good for the child, the parents, or the relationship. It tells the child that you are threatened by her feelings, or she gets the message that you don't care to understand her feelings. The child picks up on your attitude and learns that expressing or even having feelings is not okay. The child decides that the feelings that accompany the ups and downs of her daily life are not worthwhile. If this unfeeling pattern repeats itself over and over, the child quickly learns both to suppress the feelings and specially to hide them from her parents.

Even more devastating than being uncaring is responding to a child's feelings with anger messages. The fear of parents' reactions to her feelings turns a child into a feeling stuffer. On the positive side, picture what happens when a child feels free to express herself and a parent accepts her feelings.

TEACH THE CHILD TO THINK HIGHLY OF HIMSELF

Parents are the main source of a child's sense of self-worth. The child looks in the mirror and like the person he sees. He looks inside himself and is comfortable with the person he sees. He must think of this self as being someone who can make things happen and who is worthy of love. Encourage him to set goals and have high expectations of himself. In school and any other activities, he may be involved in, help him to do well and to achieve the utmost possible with his capabilities. A push of encouragement from the parent, as well as concerned interest, helps the child try hard in his daily activities. Teach him that certain things are below his dignity. These could include complaining too much, asking for things from others, getting into trouble with authorities, etc. The child will become habituated to a certain type of behavior and anything below that will seem unworthy of himself.

While each child is a little different, parents can follow some general guidelines to build kid's confidence. Self-confidence rises out of sense of competence. In other words, kids develop confidence not because parents tell them they are great, but because of their achievements, big and small.

Sure, it's good to hear encouraging words from mom and dad. But words of praise mean more when they refer to a child's specific effort or new abilities. When kids achieve something, whether it's brushing their own teeth or riding a bike, they get a sense of themselves as able and capable.

Building self-confidence can begin very early. When babies learn to turn the pages of a book or toddlers learn to walk, they are getting the "I can do it!" idea. With each new skill and milestone, kids can develop increasing confidence. For instance, if your son wants to learn how to make a peanut butter sandwich, demonstrate, set up the ingredients, and let him give it a try. Will he make a bit of a mess? Almost certainly. But try to avoid any criticism that could discourage him from trying again. If you step in to finish the sandwich, your son will think, "Oh, well, I guess I can't make sandwiches." But if you have the patience for the mess and the time it takes to learn, the payoff will be real. Someday, soon, he will be able to say, "I'm hungry for lunch, so I'm going to make my own sandwich." You might even reply, "Great, can you make me one, too?" What a clear sign of your faith in his abilities!

Beginning around age two, children can do small jobs around the house. To hold a child's interest, choose tasks the child has already shown an interest in.

Starting between ages two and four, a child can learn the concept of responsibility to self and to parents and for his personal belongings.

Once he learns a sense of responsibility for these things, a sense of responsibility to society will come naturally in the next stage of development. Encourage school-age children to make their own lunch. Besides giving them a sense of responsibility for their own nutrition, they are more likely to eat what they make. Once taught, the child can be left alone in the kitchen.

Call a job "special" and it's more likely to get done. Whatever magical ring the word *"special"* has, it sure gets results. Perhaps a child infers that "I must be special because I get a special job." A four to five-year-old can have preassigned chores, with reminders, of course. To put some order in our busy house, we announce: "It's tidy time." Try assigning one room for each child to tidy up.

Children of all ages suffer a bit of work inertia, especially as tasks wear and lose their fun appeal. But sometimes children need to learn that work comes before play. To get them started, work with them. Other jobs boys and girls love and do well when first taught alongside a parent include: washing the car, sweeping outdoor living areas and sidewalks, gardening, vacuuming, dusting and baby tending. By seven or eight, they can put in a load of laundry, and by ten, they can be doing their own laundry.

When children have jobs in the home, not only are parents relieved of some of the busywork, but children feel they are contributing to a cause. They feel useful and needed. And the energy they spend on the home becomes an investment they are making into the value system of that home.

Parents can help by giving kids lots of opportunities to practice and master their skills, letting kids make mistakes and being there to boost their spirits so they keep trying. Respond with interest and excitement when kids show off a new skill and reward them with praise when they achieve a goal or make a good effort. With plentiful opportunities, good instruction, and lots of patience from parents, kids can master basic skills, like tying their shoes and making the bed. Then, when other important challenges present themselves, kids can approach them knowing that they have already been successful in other important areas.

Sometimes, kids give up when frustrations arise. Help by encouraging persistence in the midst of setbacks. By trying again, kids learn that obstacles can be overcome. Once kids reach a goal, you will want to praise, not only the end result, but also their willingness to stick with it.

HELP YOUR CHILD TO BE MORE ORGANIZED

Most kids generate a little chaos and disorganization. Yours might flit from one thing to the next, forgetting books at school, leaving towels on the floor, and failing to finish projects once started. A few kids seem naturally organized, but for the rest, organization is a skill learned over time. With help and some practice, kids can develop an effective approach to getting stuff done.

And you are the perfect person to teach your child, even if you don't feel all that organized yourself.

For kids, all tasks can be broken down into 3 processes:

1. Getting organized: means a kid gets where he or she needs to be and gathers the suppliers needed to complete the task.

2. Staying focused: means sticking with the task and learning to say "no" to distractions.

3. Getting it done: means finishing up, checking your work and putting on the finishing touches, like remembering to put a homework paper in the right folder and putting the folder inside the backpack so it's ready for the next day.

Once kids know these steps, and know how to apply them, they can start tackling tasks more independently. That means homework, chores, and other tasks will get done with increasing consistency and efficiency. Of course, kids will still need parental help and guidance, but you probably won't have to nag as much.

Not only it is practical to teach these skills but knowing how to get stuff done will help your child feel more competent and effective. Kids feel self-confident and prouder when they are able to accomplish their tasks and responsibilities. They are also sure to be pleased when they find have some extra free time to do what they would like to do.

From teeth brushing to book reports, get started, introduce the three above mentioned methods and help your child practice it in daily life. Even something as simple as brushing teeth requires this approach, **so you might use this example when introducing the concept:**

1. *Getting organized*: Go to the bathroom and get out your toothbrush and toothpaste. Turn on the water

2. *Staying focused*: keep brushing, even if you hear a really good song on the radio or you remember that you wanted to call your friend. Concentrate and remember what the dentist told you about having healthy teeth.

3. *Getting it done*: Getting it done means finishing up and putting on the finishing touches. With teeth brushing, that would be stuff like turning off the water, putting away the toothbrush and the paste, making sure there is no toothpaste foam on your face.

With a more complex task, like completing a book report, the steps become more involved, but the basic elements remain the same.

Here is how you might walk your child through the steps:

1. **Getting organized:** Explain that this step is all about getting ready. It's about figuring out what kids need to do and gathering any necessary items. For instance: She has a book report to write. Help your child to make a list of things like choose a book. Make sure the book is Okay with the teacher. Write down the book and the author's name. Check the book out of the library. Mark the due date on a calendar.

Then help your child think of the suppliers needed: The book, some note cards, a pen for taking notes, the teacher's list of questions to answer, and a report cover. Have your child gather the supplies where the work will take place.

As the project progress, show your child how to use the list to check off what is already done and get ready for what's next. Demonstrate how to add to the list, too. Coach your child to think, "now, I did these things, what's next?

Oh yeah, start reading the book" and toad things to the list like finish the book, read over my teachers' directions, start writing the report.

2. Staying focused: Explain that this part is about doing it and sticking with the job. Tell kids this means doing what you are supposed to do, following what's on the list, and sticking with it.

It also means focusing when there is something else your child would rather be doing, the hardest part of all. Help kids learn how to handle and resist these inevitable temptations. While working on the report, a competing idea might pop into your child's head: "I feel like shooting some hoops now." Teach kids to challenge that impulse by asking themselves "Is that what I'm supposed to be doing?"

Explain that a tiny break to stretch a little and then get back to the task at hand is ok. Then kids can make a plan to shoot hoops after the work is done. Let them know that staying focused is tough sometimes, but it gets easier with practice.

3. Getting it done: Explain that this is the part when kids will be finishing up the job. Coach your child to take those important finial steps: putting his or her name on the report, placing it in a report cover, putting the report in the correct school folder, and putting the folder in the backpack so it's ready to be turned in.

Tips

Ask yourself some of the following questions: Will it be easy or hard? Is he or she already doing some of it? Is there something he or she would like to get better at? Start the conversation by using the examples. Brainstorm about what might be easier or better if your child was more organized and focused. Maybe homework would get done faster, there would be more play time, and there would be less nagging about chores. Then there is the added bonus of your child feeling proud and you being proud too. Be clear in a kind way, that you expect your kids to work on these skills and that you will be there to help along the way. Decide on one thing to focus on first. You can come up with three things and let your child choose one. Or if homework or a particular chore has been a problem, that's the natural place to begin.

Though you might not realize it, every time you take on a task, you ask yourself questions and then answer them with thoughts and actions. If you want to unload groceries from the car, you ask yourself:

Q: Did I get them all out of the trunk?

A: No. I will go get the rest

Q: Did I close the trunk?

A: Yes

Q: Where is the milk and ice cream? I need to put them away first.

A: Done, now what is next?

That kind of teaching can be a very loving gesture. You are taking the time to show your kids how to do something, with interest, patience, love, kindness, and their best interests at heart. This will make kids feel cared for and loved. Think of it as filling up a child's toolbox with crucial life tools.

Make him familiar with Stories of Great People

Children love stories, and these are a great medium for imparting valuable lessons. When the children are young and rely on parents to read to them, use the opportunity to read inspiring stories of great people. Many books for children are available these days and parents should make a good use of them. Even when reading secular stories, search your local libraries for stories that will inspire the child towards good virtues. Heroes and their heroic actions are often imprinted in the minds of the child, and this will do more to push him towards noble behavior than a lecture from the parents. Manipulate the interest in stories to gain a sense of respect and dignity for noble behavior.

Caring for the Elderly

The young of today's society, will be tomorrow's elderly. Teaching them how to honor the elderly helps bridge the gap between generations and spreads an atmosphere of love and understanding between the young and the old. Even though the elder are worthier to start a conversation, the young should take initiative toward the aged in greeting and also helping, showing kindness, visiting, advising, phoning, and treating them gently.

Similarly, giving priority to the elderly in different situations is a token of respect and honor to them.

Address your Child by Name

I can still remember my grandfather impressing on me the value of using and remembering peoples' names. This lesson has proved profitable. I remember saying good morning to him, and he would be like, "Good morning what? It was a reminder that I should say, "Good morning,

Grandpa" instead. Addressing your child by name, especially when accompanied by eye contact and touch, exudes a "you are special" message. Beginning an interaction by using the other person's name opens doors, breaks barriers and even softens corrective discipline. Children learn to associate how you use their name with the message you have and the behavior you expect.

Parents often use a child's nickname or first name only in casual dialogue, "Chloe, I like what you are doing." They beef up the message by using the full name to make a deeper impression, saying, "Chloe Hirwa, stop that!" One child I heard about refers to his whole name as his "mad name" because that's what he hears when his parents are angry at him. It has been argued that children with self-confidence more frequently address their peers and adults by name or title. Their own self-worth allows them to be more direct in their communication with others. Our three-year-old son, when he is talking to his dad on the phone, he is like: "Hi, Dad!" The addition of "Dad" impresses his dad more than an impersonal "Hi!"

Lower your voice, don't raise it

As parents, we need to show self-control and use gentle words if we want our kids to do the same. It's easy to respond with yelling or anger, but your child is looking to you and that's where you need to show self-control. Try not to over-react to personalize it. By changing the tone and volume of your voice, you can help your child to stay calm. If he is unable to calm down before helping the victim in case he/she gets into a fight or trouble, turn to him and say quietly: "I need you to calm down now, I am going to help George and when I am done I want you to be quiet."

When your child returns to you calm, feel free to thank him for calming himself down and repeat it again that it's bad to fight and bite, it hurts and his friend, George, is sad. If possible, it would be good if he says sorry to the victim.

It's also important to talk to your child about aggression during a calm moment. Explain to your child that hitting, biting, kicking and other aggressive behaviors are wrong. Remember to keep your sentences short for children up to two years. Just hold him and say, "No hitting, it's bad." You may have to repeat this rule numerous times, using the same words, until your child gets it. Another thing is to help children recognize their anger by stating: "I know you are mad, but no hitting."

Having your own Childhood buried in Obscurity from your Children

Whether you were the nastiest kid in your class, getting regular detention, or you intermittently broke windows of every house in the neighborhood, stole money from your father's wallet, drove his car without his knowledge, applied Mom's makeup when she was napping, prank-called strangers on the phone at night, or lied about your tryst at some mall with a friend, everything seedy or shady about your own youth should get hidden when you become a parent yourself.

Whether it was a nasty diaper-rash that made your infant scream in agony, one that was caused by your negligence in changing her diaper on time. Or whether it was that tight slap on the cheek of your 'terrible two' toddler when he yanked a food-laden plate off the dining table onto your lap, one that left him bawling, or the time when you didn't wash your 3 years old's plates properly and she fell ill with diarrhea for a week; no one will be able to tell your children whether you were a lousy parent when they were babies or an efficient one. Whether unintentional or deliberate, behind the veil of the past. Your toddler and minors are too young to remember when they were spanked without reason, humiliated or scolded for no fault of theirs.

TEACH YOUR CHILDREN TO TAKE CARE OF THEIR BODIES

It seems like just yesterday that you had to coax your daughter to bathe, but then she turned 11 and started spending hours in the bathroom and sizing herself up in every mirror she passes. As they approach the teen years, it's common and natural for kids to become more interested in appearances, their own and others', seemingly all of a sudden. Their bodies are going through some big changes as they grow and go through puberty. Having a healthy body image means that most of your feelings, ideas, and opinions about your body and appearance are positive. It means accepting and appreciating your body and feeling mostly satisfied with your appearance. It also means that the body is something that has to be looked after every single day. In contrast to the first three years of life, children grow gradually now. It is a time of learning how to care for their bodies, and what they learn may have much to do with self-esteem and social relationships. Boys and girls are similar in body strength and coordination.

This phase is the time to make sure your children establish habits of good nutrition and hygiene. Principles of good care and hygiene apply equally to children who have physical handicaps or mental disabilities. Whatever your child's situation, encourage your child during this period to acquire habits of self-respect, hygiene, love their bodies, and attention to his body's condition.

Developing a healthy body image happens over time. It can be influenced by experiences and shaped by the opinions and feedback of others and by cultural messages. It's good to help them develop appetites for healthy rather than junk foods.

Body image and appearance

Body image can be especially vulnerable during the preteen and teen years because appearances change so much and cultural messages that fuel dissatisfaction can be very strong. Being criticized or teased about appearance can be particularly hurtful at this age. Preteens and teens often compare their looks with others' or with media images of the "right" way to look. In cultures in which looks seem to matter so much, and ideal images are so unrealistic, it's all too common to be dissatisfied with some aspect of appearance.

But feeling too self-critical about appearance can interfere with body image. And too poor body image can hurt a teen's overall self-image too. As teens mature mentally and emotionally, they will develop a more complex self-image, one that incorporates their interests, talents, unique qualities, values, aspirations, and relationships. But during the early teen years, the image they see in the mirror makes up a big part of their self-image. And while it's true that appearance isn't everything, feeling satisfied with appearance means a lot. If you are wondering why your child suddenly seems so focused on appearance, keep in mind that preteens are:

Adapting a new reflection: Spending extra time grooming, making comparisons with friends and celebrities, and experimenting with clothing, hair, and makeup can be ways of getting to know and like the new self-reflection in the mirror.

Making a fashion statement: When preteens and teens express their taste in clothes and hairstyles, they are making statements about themselves. Experimenting with and defining their styles is one way to express their interests, personality, independence, and identity.

Finding a way to belong: Peers, groups, and cliques, which take center stage during the teen years, can also play a role in heightening young teens' concerns about appearances. Dressing a certain way might be a way of feeling included, fitting in, standing out, or belonging to a group of peers.

Boys and Image

It's not just girls who become focused on appearance. Boys might not be as vocal about it, but they can worry just as much about their looks. When your son emerges wearing pants that sag as if he hasn't quite finished getting dressed, he may, in fact, have spent hours getting them to hang at that exact angle. Feeling satisfied with appearance is not always easy.

Many kids who have positive body images become self-conscious or self-critical as they enter the teen years. It's not uncommon for preteens and teens to express dissatisfaction about their appearance or to compare themselves with their friends, celebrities, or people they see in advertisements. Most cultures emphasize the need to look just right. For everything from makeup and hair products to clothing and toothpaste, send messages that people need to look a certain way to be happy. It's hard not to be influenced by that. Body shape and size can concern them too. It's important for preteens or teens to eat nutritious foods, limit junk foods and get plenty of physical activity.

In most cases, the focus on appearance is very natural and a common part of becoming a teenager. Usually, these expressions of frustration clear up quickly and don't warrant concern, just plenty of patience, empathy, support, and perspective from parents. As preteens try on different looks, parents can help them by being accepting and supportive, providing positive messages, and encouraging other qualities that keep looks in perspective. Provide reassurance about kids' looks and about all their other important qualities. As much as they may seem not to notice or care, simple statements like "you have got the most beautiful smile" or "that shirt looks great on you" really do matter.

Compliment them on other physical attributes such as strength, speed, balance, energy, or grace. Appreciating physical qualities and capabilities helps build a healthy body image. Notice out loud all the personal qualities that you love about your kids, how generous your son is to share with his little sister, the determined way that your daughter studies for her tests, or how your son stood by his best friend. Reassure them when they express insecurity.

Be a good role model. How you talk about your own looks sets a powerful example. Constantly complaining about or fretting over your appearance teaches your kids to cast the same critical eye on themselves.

Almost everyone is dissatisfied with certain elements of their appearance but talk instead about what your body can do not just how it looks. Instead of griping about how big or small your legs are (according to your culture), talk about how they are strong enough to help you hike up a mountain.

INTIMATE RELTIONSHIPS

As your child moves into a wider and crazier social world, relationships with other people present major challenges as different people will require different relations. In the neighborhood or at school, he will meet other children whose values are quite different from his own. They will talk and act somewhat differently from him. And immediately, he is faced with making rather complex decisions. If a playmate is dishonest, should the child report it, criticize it, ignore it, or urge honesty? How does a child respond to differing religious beliefs? While acquiring effective social graces is a lifelong endeavor, this is a special period of development in which parents should teach courtesy, honesty, fidelity, mercy and good humor.

Interpersonal relationships may be divided into three basic categories: courteous, affectionate, and intimate. Children must learn the differences between these categories and what is proper within each.

a. Courteous relationships are the basis of civilized behavior: saying "please" and "thank you." Courteous attitudes and behavior enable people to live pleasantly with each other, preventing them from appearing rude and mannerless.

b. Affection is natural and is mostly associated with family relations. When affection is expressed, it should be remembered that it is more intense than courtesy, but it includes courtesy. We touch people differently when being affectionate than when being courteous. A handshake may be courteous, but holding hands is affectionate. You can teach them how to be affectionate by hugging or listening to a childish story, playing games with them, talking to and touching them gently, and telling them that you do love them. All these will play a big role in covering this particular area. In the absence of natural affection at home, the child may imitate the false affections he sees displayed by schoolmates or television actors. Often, television and movies show people being aggressive, rather than kind and affectionate. And your child might conclude that that's the way to do things if he or she isn't given a good example from home.

c. Intimate relationships are deeper and longer lasting than others and are more intense. Within such relationships are very strong emotions. To a large extent, the child feels these emotions naturally. What he or she needs to learn at this stage is how to appropriately approach and express them to others later on in life, at the proper time. You and your spouse can be your children's best examples of intimate relationships. A father teaches intimacy to his sons and daughters by how he speaks to and generally treats their mother.

In some ways, this relationship between you and your spouse is more important than the parent-child relationship in teaching your children about intimacy, as a high percentage of children learn by seeing what's being done. You have a golden opportunity to demonstrate warm, mutually respecting relationships, courteous, affectionate, and intimate—and to answer questions about them once a child is finding some areas challenging.

COUNSEL YOUR CHILDREN

To counsel your children means to listen to them, give them advice, and teach them. This is very important, for as your children mature, your words become almost as important as your example. By giving your children spoken or written instructions and advice, you can prepare them to exercise their agency wisely, answer their questions, and help them understand the things they see in the world. *Counsel* is often one way. Many times, information and feelings need to be exchanged in a council. In a *council,* we can consider a matter together with everyone being able to speak freely without fear and without feeling they need to be in an agreement in order to be accepted by others. Counsel from a parent to a child is most effective when it follows listening in a council, when a parent gets a child's viewpoint before expressing an opinion. Our children are responsible for their own behavior. Give them the opportunity to sit in council with you, however informal and spontaneous. Give them clear counsel to guide them and let them practice following that counsel. They must feel the weight of decision making and, at times, the pain of error.

Your role as a parent requires that you pass judgments on your children and correct them as necessary.

Without excusing or minimizing the problem, you can react with concern, candor, and practical steps to correct the error or help your child repent.

PROVIDE A POSITIVE EMOTIONAL CLIMATE

The emotional climate in the home establishes either a positive or a negative learning environment. Climate means "the weather you can expect in a certain place." What is the "weather" in your home? Is it warm, comfortable, and secure; or is there too much thunder, lightning, and cold? Occasionally, a teaching moment will arise out of an atmosphere of tension and anxiety, but most effective teaching moments occur in loving, peaceful, respectful circumstances, when the "feeling" is right and when the climate in a relationship is peaceful.

Share your Thoughts and Feelings

Children, like adults, need to report their efforts. They enjoy telling us of their success, but they also need the comfort that comes from telling their failures to a sympathetic listener. You also need to share your thoughts and feelings with your children but wisely. Share your goals for them and for your family. If your children know these goals, they will better be able to understand your intentions and correctly interpret your actions.

Share your values, too; you could say something like, "The most precious thing in my life is my family. This gives me the motivation to get up every morning and try to do my best."

Break the Routine

Parents need an occasional break. Because parenthood requires so much time and energy, you and your children will benefit from regular breaks in the routine. You will be better able to teach if you regularly take time to refresh yourself. Dates for mother and father; weekends with a relative or friends for the children; solitude for each family member with a book, a hobby, or a household task; and some form of recreation are very important in keeping perspective and emotional balance. You need time for yourselves, even though you are expected to invest yourselves deeply in your family.

Financial Authority

Parents control their children's movement within and outside the house. They control what they eat, what they wear, where they go, who they mingle with, and what toys or accessories they buy. This makes a parent very strong as opposed to their child, in the first 2 decades of the latter's life. Plus, children depend on their parents for money. They do not and cannot earn money. Therefore, parents have almost complete control over how they bring up their children.

TEENS AND SCHOOL

When it comes to homework, be there to offer support and guidance, answer questions, help interpret assignment instructions, and review the completed work if you are able to do that, of course. And if you can't, you may know a relative or a friend who may know more about that subject and ask for a hand if possible. But resist the urge to provide the right answers or complete assignments.

It can be difficult to see your kids stressed out over homework, especially when there is a test or important deadline looming. But you can help by teaching them the problem-solving skills they need to get through their assignments and offering encouragement as they do. As students grow more independent during these years, it can be challenging for parents to know which situations call for involvement and which ones call for a more behind- the- scenes approach. Home works get more intense and grades start to matter more.

At the same time, teens face a lot of other big changes. They are adjusting to the physical and emotional effects of puberty, while busy social lives and sports commitments gain importance, and many also take part-time jobs.

Preteens and teens do better in school when parents are involved in their academic lives. Knowing the physical layout of the school building and grounds can help you connect with your child when you talk about his or her school day.

Remember that preteens and teens also need the right amount of sleep. Bedtime difficulties can arise at this age for variety of reasons, including but not limited to homework, sport, after-school activities, texting, TV, computer, videogames as well as hectic family schedules. All these can contribute to students not getting enough sleep, and lack of sleep can make it difficult for preteens and teens to pay attention in school. It's important to have a consistent bedtime routine, especially on school nights. Schools usually cite disciplinary policies. The rules usually cover expectations, as well as consequences for not meeting the expectations, for things like student behavior, dress codes, use of electric devices, and acceptable language. The policies may include details about attendance, vandalism, cheating, fighting, bullying, etc. It's important for your preteen or teen to know what's expected at school and that you will support the school's consequences when expectations aren't met.

Parents can play a crucial role in helping teens handle these challenges and succeed in school by lending a little help, support and guidance, by knowing what problems demand their involvement and which ones require them to hang back.

Your teen may prefer to retreat to a private space to work rather than study surrounded by parents and siblings.

Apply School to the "Real World"

Talk about how what teens learn now applies outside the classroom, such as the importance of meeting deadlines, as they will also have to do in the workplace, or how topics in history class relate to what's happening in today's news. It's also a good idea to make sure your preteen or teen knows how to make a daily to-do list to prioritize tasks and manage time.

Adolescents

When children enter adolescence period between ages 13 and 19, usually, they undergo a number of physical changes, from an increase in height to a surge in hormone production. Among these, of course, are changes in attitude personality.

Adolescence can be a very confusing and puzzling time for both you and your children. Just when your children are trying to learn who they are and where they belong in the world, their bodies begin the profound physical changes of puberty. Children take on the outward appearance of adults but lack adult experience, wisdom, and responsibility.

They continue to mature emotionally and socially, but there are periods of confusion and inconsistency as they try to understand and cope with the changes in their bodies, and the accompanying social changes that lead toward adult relationships. Parents can mistakenly attribute adult characteristics to adolescents who look like adults but are largely children. They need more time and experience before being expected to act and think completely as adults.

Teenagers tend to be selective in sharing their thoughts and feelings, particularly to their parents, at this stage in their lives. Some adolescents may start to view their friends as much more important or influential than their parents and guardians, who they usually consider as overprotective. That's where a parent may start thinking that their child may be selective.

PRIVACY AND SECRECY

Privacy and secrecy shouldn't be confused. There is an important difference between secrecy and privacy. A secret is something that we should not share. Privacy is a natural and dynamic boundary based on trust and respect.

There is that age when children start to separate emotionally from parents, and it's often demonstrated physically by closing the door to their rooms. They go into their rooms, lock themselves in, and put the music on. Sometimes, the child who lock herself in may need to be given some space. With all her after-school events, other activities scheduled into her day, including her homework, she is likely to want to be alone so she can play games, chat on the phone or simply daydream. Even though giving space may be needed, locking herself in has to be limited. The child can lock herself in if she is getting dressed or when she has a special assignment that needs more concentration. There is no need to lock the door every time she is in there, and that's where the parent needs to maintain his or her regular household rules, stay connected with the child and give her plenty of support.

When children are in early adolescence, they may develop a much more challenging way of talking to you.

They want to see what they can get away with, and that's where parents need to be very responsive. If you let your child get away with a hurtful remark once, it's much harder to deal with once they turn it into a habit. If your child says something inappropriate and then says he was just joking, you have to make it clear that it's not good to joke that way. There is no need to use verbal abuse. If you know for sure that it was only a joke, you can just say: "Oh, all right, that is funny, but it's not really good joking in a mean way." Your child may use his way of joking and hurt his sibling or other people's feelings.

If you overhear your child being hurtful to a sibling or his friend, talk to him later and say, "I heard you and .... (mention the name) playing earlier today and I don't think the things you were saying were very nice." Correct him and ask him what he can say differently instead of using the annoying words. Hopefully, he will think of something. If he can't, suggest something to him. This kind of behavior is part of adolescence. Our part as parents is to correct them, since we want our children to be appropriate the next time they feel that way.

When you start to crack down on the mean joking, many kids will feel like they can't have fun at home anymore because you take everything too seriously. But yes, that's how it should be. You take hurtfulness and disrespect very seriously.

It's funny when jokes aren't disrespectful or hurtful, and it's important to talk to your children about the difference between joking and being hurtful. Whenever you can, don't miss a chance to catch your child being good. It would be a very good opportunity to teach them the difference between joking and being hurtful. Sit down with your children when things are going well and tell them how good they are. Don't just wait till things fall apart and he is angry, that won't be a good time and you may not even get any attention.

Talk to them and say, "The jokes you make, even though you say you are only kidding, are really hurtful. You have to stop being hurtful and sarcastic to others." Give your child a room to discuss what you have just told him by saying, "Do you have any question? Do you understand what I mean?"

There are some children with behavioral or social problems who have learned to use humor to deflect or compensate for their lack of social solving skills. You can't just say, "He lies because he is afraid, or he steals because he doesn't have anything." Those are excuses and they don't matter. Any bad behavior in our kids should be challenged and eliminated by teaching our kids other things. Children need some empathy while upholding the rules in combination. Acknowledging the underlying issues build deeper trust and support.

There is always a real consequence to behavior without needing to punish. Punishing tends to bring anger, not self-reflection, on the part of the punished.

TIPS

- It's important for both parents to share any plan that is developed and be on the same page, or at least be willing to support each other in the process.

- Children should learn to treat family "business" at home rather than to share it with friends or neighbors. There are situations that occur between family members that are not discussed with persons outside the family circle.

- Set limits for your children, it's an act of love. Sometimes, it can be hard to know if the limits you set are reasonable or not, especially when your children are howling that "everyone is allowed to do it!" Start from your values; be clear about the values you want to instill in your family.

- Commonly held confidences create a bond of love that encourages greater unity and develops greater loyalty among family members.

- You will have provided for them truths by which they can judge their own actions. Knowing the truth enables both parent and child to communicate more effectively. Knowing the truth takes the chance out of decision making.

Only when the truth is known is one actually making a choice; otherwise, he may be simply guessing at the course he should follow.

•Try not to personalize the misbehavior. Instead, focus on the behavior and your child's need to change. Help him, understand that the misbehavior is hurtful and worth changing.

•If you are angry, wait to talk with your child until your anger has cooled.

•Don't hand down whatever punishment comes to your mind. Sit down and think about what behavior you are trying to target, then think more clearly about what consequences would be most effective in promoting change. You know what your children hold dear. Consequences are most impactful when your child really cares either about avoiding the loss of something (video game or going to her friends overnight) or about gaining something (a car or a concert).

•Set limits with timeframes. Impose consequences that allow your child to grow and change. This will help them to experience success. You can tell your child: "If you are able to make it through this evening without fighting with your brother, you will be allowed to play your videogame for 1 more hour." Start limit settings early. It's much harder to begin setting limits when your child is a teenager.

•Don't look for validation from your child, that would be giving them too much power. Part of being a parent is setting limits and teaching better behaviors. This is a hard job, and at times, you can feel pretty alone. Keep at it! Don't feel like by setting limits, you will lose your child's love. Setting limits is an act of love. Kids need limits and count on parents to set those for them to keep them safe and help them grow.

•Express your love to your children regularly and frequently. Form family rules, supervise children's work, create learning opportunities for each child, and correct your children

SECRETIVE CHILDREN

Children, for some reasons, are not comfortable sharing details of their lives with their parents. They may not disclose their lives to their parents because they are aware how unreasonable and self-destructive their choices are. They know that their parents will reason them out of genuine concern. For a child to be secretive, it may also be the result of environment. It can be that the secretive child has been harshly treated and is building a defense against severe punishment.

Children may also keep secrets because they do not trust their rigid inflexible parents to take a reasonable stance on any issue. They have experienced disproportionate reactions and unreasonable and unilateral decisions made by parents with no scope to reason and negotiate. Such children do not only keep secrets but also indiscriminately rebel against their parents' rigidities, sometimes against their own interest. Children fear being judged harshly. They fear facing anger and rejections or being mocked. They are scared of being distrusted and emotionally abandoned.

I heard about a girl who had been sexually abused by her father since she was 13 years old. At 14, when she first told her mother about it, her mother reacted with a bitter outburst.

She blamed her daughter for trying to ruin their marriage and called her a characterless girl who fantasized about her father. The girl felt most unsafe in a place where she should have felt safest; in the care of her biological mother. She saw her mother as completely unreliable and undependable for her safety and security. Her parental home was the most threatening to her physical and emotional survival. She left home at the age of 15 and never returned back. She kept her life a secret not only from her parents but from everyone else as well, as she could not bring herself to trust anyone. This girl could not rely on her parents. This created an unbridgeable divide between them. The parents in all these cases had made some unhealthy choices and behaved inappropriately that the child felt like an "emotional orphan" and, therefore, kept her life to herself.

What we learn from this real-life story is that children need to feel emotionally safe and secure. They need to be able to trust that the reason will prevail and that negotiation is possible between them and their parents. Only such a relaxed and balanced environment will help them open up their lives to their parents and help establish a healthy relationship where there is free, frank and fearless communication.

Help your child open up to you

- **Be a role model** of effective living. Let your life be a witness and your children a witness to it. Create an environment of mutual respect with your children, where you listen attentively and empathically to all they share without any judgement.

- **Be concerned** and yet playful in your communication style so that you don't aggravate anxiety in your children when they share their concerns.

- **Create opportunities** where they can casually share with you about their lives. Activities like playing a game together that your child enjoys, cooking together, or going for a walk. Chatting till late night in the dark while the child is going to sleep provides excellent opportunities to create a comfort level to talk uninhibitedly.

- **Use opportunities** like watching a TV show with your child to initiate a discussion on a topic on which you could ask for your child's views and share your own

- **Ask questions** with open-ended sentences, questions that can't simply be answered by "yes" or "no".

- **Don't' stop** your teen from having a crush as this is normal during adolescence, talk about it in a casual and non-judgmental way.

- **Inform your teen** about the consequences of pre-marital sex, such as sexual diseases, unwanted pregnancies, and early parenthood. Let your teen decide for herself. Give her guidance, but don't make the decisions since these will only push her away from you. Sometimes, all your teen needs are a listening ear and a shoulder to cry on.

- **When your child confesses** to a wrongdoing, do not criticize or say, "I told you." Instead, ask your child how he plans to turn things around and what help he/she expects from you.

- **Make them feel important:** Consult them on family matters. Let them feel they are important members of the family and have a part to play in the growth and well-being of the family.

- **Go out as a family:** Take family trips rather than allowing your children to always go out only with their friends. Let your children be around family and friends from whom you want them to pick up their values. Always remember that your children will become who they spend most of their time with.

So, watch their company and above all, give them your company whenever it's possible. One of the important things that parents must teach their children is to choose good company and to avoid bad company, as children are always influenced by the company they keep. Bad behavior can easily be transmitted through bad company.

Teach your children to choose righteous and serious friends in their lives, who will help them to make good use of their time.

Praise them: Praise is a powerful tool with children, especially in front of others. Children feel a sense of pride when their parents praise them and will be keen to perform other good deeds. However, praise must be limited to deeds of moral values.

• **Avoid humiliation:** Similarly, do not humiliate them in front of others. Children make mistakes. Sometimes, these mistakes occur in their efforts to please the parents. If you are unhappy with your children, tell them in private.

• **Responsibility:** Give them chores to do in line with their age. Convince them that they are performing an important function and you will find them eager to help you out again.

• **Don't spoil them:** Children are easily spoiled. If they receive everything they ask for, they will expect you to oblige on every occasion. Be wise in what you buy for them. Avoid extravagance and unnecessary luxuries. Take them to an orphanage or poor area once in a while so they can see how privileged they are.

• **Apologize when you hurt them:** Saying sorry for your mistakes will exalt your ranks and teach your children to do the same. For example, saying to your toddler: "I'm sorry I yanked your arm so hard on the road. I was afraid of the cars passing by you and was just being careful. I did not mean to be so harsh."

• **Admit it to your child when you are wrong and they are right:** Children can help their parents a lot. If the parent has a humble attitude instead of a *"know it all"* one, they can pave the way for positive learning on both sides. More importantly, winning an argument should never be your goal just because you have rights over your children. Say *"you are right"* to them when they are. That way, you will be teaching them by example to give you the respect which you supposedly deserve as well.

• **Work hard with your first child:** Everything that you want to achieve in your children, do it with the first child. If you work hard with the first child, the second child will follow suit. While you are working with the first, that little baby on your lap (your second), would have picked up everything that you are teaching the first one and by the time you need to teach him/her, she would have already learnt them.

DEFIANT CHILD

There are those parents who live the kind of situation every day when they have a defiant (difficult) child. But what is going on in the child's mind when he is fighting with the parent? Although it may feel like he hates you, that's usually far from the truth. They are things that can tangle up their emotions and behavior. Those things can dominate a person's thought processes throughout their entire lives.

•**Injustice:** This is being commonly used by children. Have you realized that many kids see things as being unfair? Telling her to go to bed when it's bedtime and when she is watching her favorite cartoon is unfair to her. The danger is that once they label something as "not fair," they feel like they don't have to follow the rules or honor your expectations. This is pretty common in our society. We all use wrong thinking to justify doing things we know are risky or unhealthy. People use wrong thinking every day to gamble, lie, steal, or cheat. Children use their wrong thinking to avoid taking responsibility.

•**The victim stance:** Some kids see themselves as victims all the time and in almost every situation. What they do is to try rejecting the idea that they are responsible for anything.

You will ask them a question and they have always got a sad story to tell. Part of that sad story is who they blame for not meeting their responsibilities. That's because when you are a victim, you blame other people. Your children blame you or they blame somebody else.

There is a sad story, and there is a behavior story. The sad story is your child playing the victim; the behavior story is what your child did to other people or property. As parents, we have to focus on the behavior story. Children can sound like blaming their teacher for not explaining well the lesson, and that would be an excuse for not doing their homework. Having homework done is a child's responsibility. It's not the teacher's job to get along with the child, but it's the child's job to get along with their teacher.

There is a way of thinking about things in which relationships with people in authority are simply vehicles your child uses to go around the rules. When the child uses this thinking in his mind, relationships are designed to help him get around rules, expectations, and responsibilities.

So, he is like, "If I have a relationship with you (since I am your baby), you are going to let me stay up past bedtime, play my favorite game and sleep late at night." To your child, rules and rights of others are seen as obstacles in relationships.

•**Pride in Negativity**: Defiant kids often take a lot of pride in their knowledge of unhealthy, secretive things. Those kids, in general, will see negative behavior as a solution to their problem; in other words, "Pride in negativity" means self-esteem and identity from negativity.

It's important to remember that children believe in the wrong thinking they are using. As a parent, get a corrective response that challenges or refuses their wrong thinking. These wrong thinking are part of everyday life. You will find that people use them all the time. You might find yourself using them too. Children, especially teens, use these thinking to avoid doing things that are difficult for them and that's dangerous. Adolescence is one of the most critical times in our children's development. It's good for them to learn how to solve life's problems, not avoid them by using excuses, manipulation, or lies.

RUDENESS AND RESPECT

We all know that a sense of humor is vital. When your child is young, up until the age of six or so, you can just correct them when they are joking in an inappropriate way or using a curse word; the kind of things that you would say to a young child is: "We don't joke by saying hurtful things. And that was hurtful." If your child says it again, you should go ahead and give him a consequence. Joking is good. Joking is a break, a rest from the ongoing seriousness and striving, and it is a little relaxation. The kind of joking which is forbidden is that which leads to hurt feelings, generates hatred and causes people to lose respect and dignity.

Disrespectful & Aggressiveness

The reason behind disrespectful behavior includes the perfectly normal and healthy process of your child growing up and away from his identity as a young child. While it may be healthy and normal in some cases, disrespectful behavior is not something to ignore. Parents have to role model better behavior for their kids. They are watching you, even if they don't seem like they care about what you do. Children watch us for a living. Don't be surprised if your child follows suit.

Few situations are more difficult to deal with than having a child who is aggressive toward other children. It can be embarrassing as well as frightening when your child bites, hits, scratches or kicks to get his way.

It's common for young children to engage in this type of behavior at various points in their development. However, when it becomes very frequent or seems to be their consistent way of reacting to something they don't like, then it's time to help them change their behavior.

Initially, between the ages of 1 to 2 years and sometimes even younger, children find it extremely hard to communicate their needs to their parents, caregivers and other children. I realized this behavior in my first child when she was in that age. She would hit another child playing with a toy she wanted. For older children between the ages of 3 to 6, such behaviors may be a self-defense, lack of adult supervision, extreme frustration, anger, mirroring the aggressive behaviors of other children around them, or the result of never having learned appropriate and non-aggressive ways of communication when they were faced with a difficult situation.

Check if your child becomes too aggressive to one particular friend, to you or tend to be aggressive with whoever he is with. If it's one child in particular, it may probably be caused by lack of clear rules before play begins. If he becomes aggressive when there is too much going on, maybe he is over-stimulated.

If you observe the situations carefully, you will likely notice patterns. You also need to check how aggressiveness is being expressed, if it's through angry words or through physical aggressiveness. By finding out all this, you are on your way to help your child become more aware of his aggressive feelings and teach him to calm down. Consequences also work well in this situation. Consequences are imperative to ending aggressive behavior in young children. They teach your child that all behaviors have a consequence, whether good or bad, and will help him make better choices in future.

Young children are not able to hear long explanations of why their behavior was offensive. A simple yet firm statement such as "It's bad to bite" should be enough while you twin your attention to the victim. It's not good yelling at your child while attending to the victim, forcing your child to apologize immediately or continuing to talk to other parents around you about how embarrassed or angry you are. If your child cannot calm down, remove him or her from the situation without getting angry yourself.

BULLYING

The characteristics of a bully include impulsive, dominating behavior, a low frustration level, a lack of empathy, a need to be the center of attention, and unhealthy attitudes towards violence and its consequences. Although many believe insecurity and self-loathing are at the root of a bully's problem, usually, the opposite is true. Bullies tend to be overconfident. They portray a fearless nature and physical strength, qualities often admired by their peers.

Bullying behavior is typically classified into three categories:

1. **Physical bullying**: Physical intimidation, hitting, kicking, pushing, choking and/or spitting.

2. **Verbal bullying**: Name-calling, threats, taunting, teasing, rumor spreading, and slander.

3. **Social bullying**: Intentional exclusion and isolation from social and peer group activities by manipulation and rumor spreading.

Many factors within a child's environment can contribute to their aggressive behavior, including family, peer group, neighborhood, society, and school. Children who bully are more likely to experience violence or neglect in the home and have less supervision and involvement from their parents.

Children picked-on by older siblings tend to become bullies themselves. Others see bullying as means to gain acceptance, friendship, and popularity. The victim of a bully is typically a child who appears insecure or cautious, a child that rarely defends or retaliates when confronted, and/or a child lacking in social skills or physical strength. Unfortunately, since bullies lack compassion, children with physical disabilities are also prey, and so are overweight children and those that wear glasses or have a speech impediment. However, any child can be the victim of a bully. Bullies will also challenge popular children in an attempt to gain more popularity. Sometimes, it is just a matter of being in the wrong place at the wrong time. The bully needs an audience. Therefore, bullying primarily occurs on school grounds and is played out in front of a group. Lunchrooms, playgrounds, hallways, locker rooms, and bathrooms are prime areas for confrontation.

The consequences of bullying are many. Children will go to great lengths to avoid being the victim of a bully. If they are not prepared in a positive way, they will naturally resort to negative ways of coping such as cutting class, feigning illness, poor grades and social withdrawal. For a child repeatedly victimized by a bully, humiliation, fear, anxiety, and depression are constant companions that can lead to harmful, shocking, unexpected behavior from another shy and timid child.

Victims may feel ashamed and tend to view themselves as failures. They are more prone to stress-related illnesses such as headaches and stomach aches. In extreme cases, the victim of a bully can experience severe depression and entertain thoughts of suicide.

Lack of safety is a top concern to young people, and bullying is a real and constant threat. When a child's sense of security is compromised, the child usually responds by taking the role of bystander, even if the victim is a friend. This burdens a child and may cause him or her to harbor feelings of guilt because they did nothing to stop or prevent the bullying. Reasons for not reporting bullying or helping a friend in trouble include fear of retribution and exclusion, as well as other personal consequences.

A lack of security deeply damages the learning environment and process. It may result in the disruption of the classroom and preoccupy students.

It can also inhibit a child's creativity and self-expression. Subsequently, this leads to poor attention spans and academic achievements suffer.

Prepare your child for the Bully

Teach your child to walk tall and to maintain eye contact. Body language is important in all aspects of your child's life. Portraying a positive, self-confident stature will help your child cope in many areas. Teach your child to accompany the confident posture with positive, self-affirming thoughts that validates his or her rights as a person. These affirmations will aid your child in speaking up without provoking a bully, and very well serve to defuse the situation. The element of surprise can make the bully take a step back. Bullies like easy prey. A joke, a flip comment, or a question is an unexpected response to harassment, and might be just enough to make the bully think his actions aren't delivering the desired outcome. Help your child to identify role models. Encourage your child to read stories that inspire. Share some time with your child and point out how strength of character and perseverance can achieve positive outcomes without resorting to violence or force.

Friendships are very important. If your child has difficulties making or maintaining friends, intervene and help. Friendships are a protection against bullying. Observe and identify children that might have things in common with your child and arrange a visit. Encourage your child to join activities that will build strength and confidence.

Bullying has become a pervasive and serious form of harassment in many schools. Dr. DAN Olweus, a professor of psychology and leading expert on bully-victim problems, reports that one child in ten is regularly attacked either verbally or physically by bullies. Elementary school-age children are the most frequent target of bullying by older students. The best way to safeguard your children from becoming a victim of a bully is to teach them how to be assertive. This involves encouraging your children to express their feelings clearly, to say no when they feel pressured or uncomfortable, to stand up for themselves verbally without fighting, and to walk away in more dangerous situations. Bullies are less likely to intimidate children who are confident and resourceful.

The following are the traits common to bullies:

1. They are concerned with their own pleasure rather than thinking about anyone else.
2. They want power.
3. They are willing to use other people to get what they want.
4. They find it difficult to see things from someone else's perspective.

Tips for helping children deal with bullies

- Teach your children early on to steer clear of youth with bullying behavior.
- Teach your children to be assertive rather than aggressive or violent when confronted by a bully.
- Instruct them to walk away and get help from an adult in more dangerous situations.

Keep communication lines open with your children. Encourage your children to share information about school and school-related activities. Respond to your children's concerns and fears with patience, love, and support.

RUN AWAY

Becoming pregnant is the most popular reason that (or used to) makes girls run away from their homes in Africa. There was a time in Rwanda (my home country) back in days when getting pregnant before getting married was believed to be a shame and an embarrassment to the girl's family. Once her family gets to know about it, they could throw her to an Island called IJWI, a place close to Congo, which was well known for having a lot of wild beasts. No one would easily survive after being thrown there. Rwandan women were (are) believed to be so beautiful. Congolese men would wait on the other side of the Island, waiting to rescue the beauty that may be thrown and make her his wife.

In Africa, many girls have suffered from the stigma associated with pregnancy outside marriage. The people around the community tease and put them to shame.

Girls and young women who get pregnant out of marriage are often disowned by their parents or forced to marry the man who impregnated them, who is sometimes much older than the girl. This makes most girls run away from their families or societies.

There are those girls, if they are lucky enough to be in school, that are sometimes squeezed into a dark and crumbling mud huts, or are taught under trees when the weather permits, or have to walk multiple miles to a neighboring village. And there are those who can't attend school at all due to various reasons, including poverty, which, in most cases, is one of the reasons why they get pregnant at such a young age. There are children who use running away as a problem-solving skill in a response to rules or limits that are being set in the home. Running away is like any other action. Kids may run away from home because of a variety of reasons. It could be a stressful situation your child is under, a fear of getting consequences for something they did, like drug or alcohol abuse, fear, anger, feeling of failure, or because they became pregnant and they are afraid of their parents' disapproval.

HELP YOUR TEENAGERS TO HAVE WHOLESOME SOCIAL EXPERIENCES

Before adolescence, children generally associate with others of the same sex. Now they should learn to interact properly with members of the opposite sex. Adolescents should begin to notice each other and should find pleasure in social relationships. Their task is to refine their social skills so that they can kindly and considerately support one another. While helping your teenagers become effective in their social experiences, do not make the mistake of distrusting them.

Many adults fall into this trap because young people tend to be more eager than wise. But there are many ways in which you can help your children to be trustworthy. But they also need to learn by experience. Make sure that family rules are clear and that rewards and punishments are consistent and prompt. Adolescents will question many things they formerly accepted, so now is a time to offer reasons for family rules. You may want to explain that a curfew hour of midnight on Fridays is based upon parental knowledge and judgment, not upon opposition to dating or social enjoyment. It is often helpful to have family councils where you and your children agree on family rules and rewards and punishments before situations arise where they are needed.

Each member of the family is responsible for their own actions and behaviors, each person is responsible for following rules and expectations. Each person is responsible for how they respond to stressful or frustrating situations. In most cases, we as parents don't take responsibility for our own actions. Without accountability in place, that's when we start blaming others for our actions, refusing to follow rules we find unfair. If your child breaks the rules by calling his siblings rude names or by being physically aggressive with them, he may be in the habit of blaming them for his actions. You will hear things like: "He couldn't move out of the way, so I pushed him." Your child should know that no matter what happened first, everyone is responsible for their own behavior, and everyone has to follow the rules.

When all members of your family start becoming accountable to each other, your children will have a clear understanding of the rules and will be much more motivated to uphold them. They will even try to follow the rules when they don't want to do so because they will know that they will be held responsible for their choices. This will help them to be organized and to live in peace with others, not only at home but also outside and in their future.

Prepare your teenagers for the changes that will accompany puberty

You should prepare your children for the changes that accompany puberty before these changes actually begin. *Puberty* is the process by which hormones cause the body to change in ways that make procreation possible. These changes mark the passage from childhood to adulthood. The processes are clean, good, and divinely mandated. There is no certain schedule, but this process usually begins between ages eleven and thirteen and can continue through adolescence and into early adulthood. At puberty, the girl begins to menstruate, her hips broaden, her breasts develop, body hair grows under her arms and in her pubic area, and she may gain weight.

The boy begins to create seminal fluid and sperm cells. His shoulders broaden, his muscles expand, his voice deepens, and he gets taller and heavier. Body hair grows under the arms, on the face, and in the pubic region. If your daughter's menstrual cycle is painful or excessive in length or volume, she should see a physician. Her mother should help her determine the most comfortable type of sanitary aid and teach her about proper hygiene and deodorizing. There are often mood changes connected with menstruation, but ordinarily, they are moderate and should not interfere with normal activities.

Girl's First Menstruation

Most girls, when they get their first menstruation, they know nothing about it. Most of them are afraid, and sometimes think something bad is happening to them. Unfortunately, most parents find it difficult to discuss this issue with their daughters. Some who would want to discuss it do not know how to present it. Guidance in a girl's first menstrual experience can be presented in an interesting, friendly, and easy way to understand.

Changes in girls start earlier than in boys. However, reproductive development of girls begins with the start of menstruation. Menstruation is the monthly flow of blood through the birth canal or the vaginal passage of female. Many refer to it as *'menses'* or *'period'*. When a girl menstruates, it means that her body is growing up. It shows that the girl can get pregnant and have a baby. Even though it doesn't mean they are ready to have children, if she indulges in sex, she can get pregnant.

Most girls begin to menstruate at about thirteen years, some start as early as nine years and others as late as seventeen years. If a girl does not begin menstruation before the age of seventeen, she may need to see a doctor for help.

After having the period, the girl will most likely want to start by using a sanitary napkin or pad. They are simple to use but the process can be a little teasing.

Choose a pad of the appropriate thickness and absorbency. For the *'thickness'*, the lighter the period, the thinner the pad. However, absorbency of pads has improved; some thinner pads can be quite absorbent. Most girls change their pads when they need to hit the girls' room, but sometimes the desire can strike at empty bladder times. Whatever it is, girls find the nearest bathroom, remove any wrappers or boxes from the pad. The wrappers can be discarded but it's a good idea to use them to dispose the used pad that is being replaced. No one wants to look at a used pad in the trash, and it can never ever be thrown in the toilet, it could flood.

To put it on, stick the adhesive part to the pantie, for the pad to be directly beneath the vagina. If the pad got wings, fold those around the outside of the pantie so that they stick, and keep the pad from moving around, which will be way more comfortable and feel a lot more natural. If the pad is itchy or irritating the skin, it should be removed and replaced with a different kind.

The pad should be changed every few hours as mentioned above, part of this depends on how heavy the flow is. Not only will changing often give peace of mind, but odors won't start worsening either. Although it may feel strange at first, the pad will generally not be visible. It will follow the curve of the body and be well hidden. A check routine is necessary, especially on heavy days. It won't get long to know how often the pad needs to be changed, and there's no need to run to the bathroom every half an hour, but checking every 2 hours will be fine, otherwise, the need to change can be felt.

During menstruation, development of the breasts with nipples becoming larger and darker, growing hair at the underarm and genital areas, skin problems like acne, eczema and others, hips broaden, body curves become more pronounced to give rounder shape, and growth of genital—these are all signs that the adolescent girl is maturing sexually and becoming a woman.

When a girl reaches puberty, once every month or 28 days on the average, the womb prepares itself for pregnancy. The cycle begins with the building up of the lining of the uterus with soft tissue and rich blood supply. The lining of the uterus comes out along with blood through the vagina. The bleeding usually lasts for four to seven days every month.

After a Girl starts having her Period

•During puberty, 'hormones' are produced in the body, and these hormones cause emotional changes, by feeling happy at one moment but sad or easily angered the next moment.

• A girl who is in her period should bathe at least twice a day. Her soaked pad should be changed every few hours.

•She should always carry an extra pad in a bag when going to school or anywhere else; this will help her to change when necessary.

•The symptoms may announce menstruation several days before the bleeding starts, such as waist and abdominal pains, loss of appetite, nervousness, inability to concentrate, tenderness of the breasts, etc. Even though some of the girls or women do not feel any pain during their periods, some do experience severe pain and sometimes take medicine to reduce the pain. Sometimes, getting enough rest, exercise, relaxation and nourishing foods relieve those symptoms.

•At the beginning of menstruation, the flow of blood may be irregular, but continued irregular flow may mean there is a health problem and the best thing to do is to seek medical attention.

• It's important to stay hygienic during periods. Washing hands always doubly well when changing pads and clean up down there (unscented sanitary wipes can come in handy for this part). The less mess, the fewer germs, the healthier.

Teenagers desires for physical intimacy

The so-called sex drive in humans is not entirely the chemical or instinctive compulsion to mate like in animals. Rather, from the time we are born, we each need to be physically and socially nurtured. The changes of puberty permit us to experience remarkably heightened pleasures of touch and arousal. But we have the agency to control the emotions and behaviors leading up to intentional sexual arousal. We can control when, where, how, and with whom we express our sexuality.

Your teenagers will face great pressures to express their sexual feelings in sinful ways. No matter how decent the family environment, there will be external indecent influences on the young person. School associates, television, movies, and magazines are filled with sensual, malicious and provoking pictures and ideas. Your teenagers will be tempted to have sexual relations with others before the right time. They will see others doing so through some schoolmates or through television. Teach your children that they will find joy in their bodies when they use them virtuously.

Your children will see in movies and in the lives of some people around them those who seem to be able to break the rule you are giving them and still live a happy, prosperous lives. Make sure they understand that they must not be misled by appearances.

They cannot expect to break the rule in one area of their lives and have the rest of their lives unaffected.

If anyone engages in sex and gets pregnant or get sexually transmitted diseases, they should not be shunned away, rather they should be helped.

Good behavior leads to self-esteem, peaceful feelings, and knowledge of right; carnal behavior leads to misery, unhappiness, and loss of the desire to do right. This applies to all areas of life, and there are no exceptions. Set the example of good behavior in every aspect of your life. Obey the traffic laws, live within your income, keep your house and yard neat and attractive, and be moderate in your dressing. As you do these things, you will show your children examples.

GOING OUT

As a child grows, he often requests to go out with friends. A parent should be in full control as to where the child is going, with whom, and for how long. Allowing the child to go whenever and wherever he pleases is sure to invite trouble. Some of the outings are the dancing parties. If it's a properly conducted dancing party, it can be good. It provides an opportunity to spend a pleasant evening with many people to the accompaniment of music. It can create and develop friendships which will be treasured in later years. Alternatively, it can become a restricting experience.

Teenagers love parties. Well-ordered dances provide favorable places, pleasing times, and auspicious circumstances in which to meet new people and to enlarge circles of friends. They can be an open door to happiness. In an evening of pleasurable dancing and conversation, one can become acquainted with many splendid young folks, every one of whom has admirable traits and may be superior to any one companion in at least some qualities. Here, partners can begin to appraise and evaluate, noting qualities, attainments, and superiorities by comparison and contrast.

Such perceptive friendships can be the basis for wise, selective, occasional dating, for those of sufficient age and maturity, this to be followed later in proper timing by steady dating, and later by proper courtship which culminates in a happy, never-ending marriage.

On the other hand, dancing can encourage improper intimacies by its exclusiveness. When guiding your teenagers in their choices of activities, help them avoid these undesirable activities by providing alternatives.

Teach them that we can enrich each other's lives. The highest purpose of anyone's mortal life is to bless others. Each of us has some gift or talent that, when developed properly, will bless someone else. As you plan activities, remember also that the tendency of the world is to equate happiness with material things. Do not plan or support activities that require you or your teenagers to spend very much money. Also, make sure that youth activities do not take your teenagers away from family duties or outings. Your family should always be the major source of friendship and support for your teenagers.

Adolescence is a time of great physical, social, and emotional power. With your help, they can have the good experiences that will allow them to mature into responsible adults. When youthful boys and girls are given family, they readily develop a sense of responsibility.

TEACHING CHILDREN ABOUT SEX

President Brigham said: "Parents should never drive their children, but lead them along, giving them knowledge as their minds are prepared to receive it" (*Discourses of Brigham Young, sel. John A. Windtsoe, Salt Lake City: Desert Book co., 1941, p. 208*).

In matters of human sexuality, honesty and accuracy are important. Your children will hear of this subject in various ways. Nowadays, people talk about sex all the time: in the news, in advertisements, in casual conversations, etc.

The world we live in now is where drugs and violence are commonplace, where chances of sexual perversion and molestation are increasing, and where the tentacles of danger reach into our households through the internet. The only safety we can provide to our children is healthy values, which empower them when they are out in the real world.

For such communication to take place on a sustained basis, our children need to allow us to be a part of their world. This can only happen when they believe that we, as parents, are trustworthy, balanced, rational, loving and are ourselves living effective lives.

Children think that sex is something they should never talk about, rather than realizing that sex is something that can be talked about privately with those they trust. It's essential that your children feel comfortable speaking to you about their private thoughts, feeling and actions because they trust you. To many, sex is physically and emotionally sensitive, and children often feel vulnerable initiating such conversations.

Although learning about sexuality can be traumatic for children, especially when what they are taught at home conflicts with some of what they encounter elsewhere. Teaching children about sexuality can be a bit challenging, too. But this topic can be introduced from an early age, to give yourself a good start. You might say to your young child: "Your sexual parts are your 'privates'. No one should touch your privates, that's why we call them privates." You might go on to explain that it's not appropriate to show your privates to others, unless there is a special reason, such as during medical exams. You may add that when we touch our privates, we need privacy—like when you wash yourself in the bathroom or dress yourself in the bedroom. Be cautious to keep your own bodies and intimate sexual relations private. Children do not need to see or hear details of your private sexual life.

You have heard about women that got pregnant with their babies after being raped.

In most cases, in their homes, sexuality is treated as a harmful act, and men are identified as hurtful and aggressive perpetrators.

I have heard about a young man in his early twenties, who was born to a raped mother. His feelings about sex and sexuality conflicted and tormented him. He grew up with very negative feelings about his own sexuality. He firmly believed it was impossible for a woman to experience anything sexually pleasing with a man. His inner conflict about sex rendered him impotent. He got to know that he has a problem after realizing the problem of his erectile dysfunction. He needed counseling to overcome his negative views of himself and his sexuality that he learned at home.

After being counseled, he slowly confronted his related negative body image and his doubts about intimacy. By working to understand those feelings, he came to understand his self-loathing, which was caused by stories he had internalized from what he heard about men from his mother. Whether his mother knew it or not, she had impaired his relationships and sexual development, both through distress with and contempt for men. Being counseled helped him to develop a positive self-image.

Situations like these are indeed complicated and we cannot blame this boy's mother for her problems or for the impact it had upon his son, as herself must have been doing her best to heal from a devastating trauma while raising an unexpected son alone.

Maybe her son also kept on asking about his father that he never saw or hear about, which may have pushed her to tell him the reality. We can see from this story how easily pain can be passed on. We can also learn from this story how a parent's general attitude toward the other sex can play a large role in the formation of a child's identity and confidence. This boy's mother's contempt for men created within her son a feeling of self-contempt because of all that he had heard about his gender, and he felt guilty and condemned for being a man.

You can hear such terrifying stories about children born from raped mothers in my country Rwanda, where women were raped during the 1994 genocide. The worst part of some is when you hear about those women who got raped after her rappers had killed the members of her family, in her eyes, or those who got raped in front of their own children before they got killed. Imagine her facing her rapper who killed her children and husband or other members of the family, and at the same time knowing that he is the father of the now living child of hers! It's a nightmare!

Imagine what the child she gave birth to would feel after hearing that story, maybe not from the mother but from someone else. It's not easy at all but no matter what our backgrounds, we have the power as parents to help our children gain a positive understanding of themselves.

Parental attitudes have a huge impact on children, whether positive or negative, conscious or unconscious.

Through doing our own work and passing on the self-love and gaining healthy perspective, as parents, we can help our children avoid many unforeseen and destructive consequences that may loom down the road.

What about children whose parents are divorced? Children can be casualties of their parents' divorce. Emotional distress from the parents' divorce can affect them throughout their whole life. The good news is that the impact of divorce for your children is within your control. It's what you will do with your children during your divorce or after that most significantly affects their outcomes. Because divorce evokes powerful emotions in parents, they may forget the impact of describing or implying all of the opposite sex as sick, evil, disgusting or some other negative terms. They often rationalize that children can distinguish between their anger and their actual beliefs.

Your children will remember your anger and your judgements about the opposite sex, especially because these feelings come across so much more powerfully and sincerely than what you might say in rational explanations to make them feel better.

At times, when you honestly feel that your emotions are getting the better of you, find someone in your family who is of the child's same gender who can support and develop the trusting relationship that is necessary to communicate with your child experientially about sexuality—a godparent, a grandparent, aunt, uncle or close friend.

Some children will seek an explanation that includes conception and birth; others will not. Frequently, there are language or vocabulary problems about sex long before the child actually wonders about the sexual process in any detail. If you have open communication, not forcing the issue, you can help the child understand all he needs to know for his age.

To obtain technical details of all the marvelous phases of human development, you and your children may want to study a medical text.

You may need to start by having a notion of how the conception occurs. After the woman's ovary releases an egg, which enters her fallopian tubes, millions of sperm are released into the woman's vagina through the man's penis. These cells propel themselves up in the vagina, into the uterus, and toward the egg. If one sperm enters the egg, conception has occurred. The egg then travels down the fallopian tubes and attaches to the lining of the uterus (womb). This lining and the egg pass off monthly through menstruation unless the egg is fertilized by a male sperm cell.

The one cell of a single fertilized egg begins to change and to multiply dramatically. In its earliest stages, the developing organism is called a *zygote;* then it is an *embryo*. After that, it is often called a *fetus*. Within the womb, the fetus which develops into a baby is protected somewhat from noise, disease, or injury by the amniotic fluid. About nine months later; the baby has matured enough to live outside the mother's body as an infant.

All this is to help your children to understand some of the questions he asks himself or hear from his friends, and also understand the proper nature of the family and of our relationships with others and the values that influence those relationships, the true roles with regard to each other.

Parents and families are critical in sex education. Their behaviors and efforts to build meaningful connections set the stage for the child's understanding of relationships. Regardless of the family's formation, the witnessing of children's parental attitudes creates both apprehensions and confidences about relationships and sexuality. The family role remains essential in building a healthy and grounded experience for children's relational and sexual development.

COURTSHIP AND MARRIAGE

Courtship allows your children to practice in a limited way the roles necessary in marriage. Proper courtship is the phase during which your children will decide whether or not to marry a specific person. Courtship is a time to discover if partners are socially and emotionally matching. Selfish, unkind habits may be hidden temporarily, but they will inevitably break through. Unselfishness, respect, generosity, and kindliness may waver under the tension of courtship or the stresses of marriage but will also inevitably break through and dominate.

As many of you know, there are too many heartrending situations where couples ignored social and emotional danger signs during courtship in the vain hope that things would improve after marriage. It is far better to break up an engagement than a marriage. There is no comparison between the temporary annoyance of calling off a wedding and the enduring pain of a broken marriage. It should not begin before your children have nearly reached maturity.

Following childhood, a youth has other obligations besides choosing a mate or having a 'good time.' He must determine first of all what kind of character he will develop.

He must decide what his trade or profession will be, and if and when he chooses a wife, how he will support her and the children. In proper courtship, the partners must recognize that their first responsibilities are to encourage each other in good behavior and to sustain and support each other in good desires and ambitions. The young man will do anything to protect the young lady as a man. When couples respect each other enough to practice virtue in every aspect of their courtship, they lay a foundation likely to withstand the most serious assaults during the marriage. The challenges and rewards of marriage come as two people learn to be one. It is not an easy task for two previously separate individuals to learn what is needed to become physically, socially and emotionally one while retaining healthy self-esteem.

Advice to a daughter that is getting married

Getting married is one of the biggest decisions of a young woman's life. And in most cases, every parent has something to tell her daughter before her wedding; not only the parents who wish to give their advice to the bride to be as a package that will help her in a new journey, but also relatives, mostly aunties and big sisters, and also friends, perhaps those who got married already.

From my experience, and considering what I have been hearing from hundreds of different couples, your daughter who is getting married should know this:

A good marriage is made. They don't just fall from heaven or off the pages of a romance novel. Unfortunately, many couples still believe that everything will be just fine after the wedding. Well, maybe the wedding will be absolutely lovely but the hard work of the marriage will be right after. A married woman should understand a man's needs and bear in mind that these needs are different to their own. It sounds very 1950's, but make sure to keep the husband happy and remember that they are wired differently to women. Men don't often like to talk about their feelings. Your husband's goals are also incredibly important, so work with him to help him achieve them. Be your own person. Keep your own hobbies, interests, and friends.

This goes both ways—let him go to his friends to watch the game and use that time to do something you want to do.

Men live in the now, whereas woman hold onto the past. If there is a disagreement, guys tend to say their piece and move on. Women tend to hold on to the moment and it can last for days. Women can then lash out at something trivial, not related to the original argument and the guy can't understand why and thinks that the woman is overreacting, but his wife is only just carrying the hurt from the argument from days before. She feels it has not been rectified but he has already forgotten it. She needs to realize that he is totally over that last argument and has forgotten it.

Unless she feels it's still important and needs to be discussed, she should be prepared to bring it up in a non-threatening way to work through it. Don't stew on it. Don't bring up the past. Last week's fight was last week. If he breaks your favorite mug and you forgive him, let it go.

Advice to a son that is getting married

Tell him that marriage is serious. Mates are great, but his wife should come first. Women change and tend to be more emotional than men, so don't react too strongly.

And for mothers, everyone knows how mothers are a very important figure in their sons' life.

The link between a mother and son is one of the most precious and special relationships a woman shares. When her little man grows up and starts paying attention to "other girls," a mom can experience a little jealousy and possessiveness, hence, the popular idea that "no girl is perfect for my son." But if you don't want to become the kind of mother that won't let her son go, realize that one day another woman will come along that your son will love with all his heart. To keep a great relationship with your child once he is married (and to have a strong relationship with your future daughter in law), make sure your son hears the following straight from your lips:

- **I love you**: Your son needs to know you love him and support him. Hearing this from you ensures he knows you trust his decision to marry this woman he loves so much. Also, make sure your son knows you will love his wife as your own child.

- **I will always be your mother**: Even when he is married and has children of his own, you will still be his mother. You will look after his wife and their family, but you will also realize that he has his own home and life to look after. Let him know you will always be there for him when he needs your help and love.

- **The best way to love his children** will be to openly express his love to his wife.

A few years ago, an old friend and his wife told me a story that I know helped them establish a strong and lasting marriage. When this man was ready to propose, he proudly showed his mother the engagement ring he had purchased for his girlfriend. His mother said, "She deserves much better than this, you can try a little harder for her." The young man returned the ring and worked harder to get the best ring he could for his bride-to-be, and then proposed. Throughout their marriage, his mother would say the same thing on any other similar situation: "You can try a little harder for her." This has helped them throughout their whole life together. Tell your son to try a little harder for your daughter in law. After all, she will be the queen of his heart, so he will be fighting for a good cause; and fighting for his woman is one of the things that makes him a real man.

Advice to a daughter or a son that is getting married

This goes to any of your children that is getting married: Nothing is more important in a marriage than the relationship between husband and wife. When other things become more important, such as careers, children and personal pursuits, trouble sets in. The relationship should be made top of all priorities. When this is done, the marriage will flourish. Marrying people should know that it's necessary to make sure he or she is accountable for the part he/she plays in the relationship, good or bad.

When you are in denial about your part in the relationship, then you are no better than a child flinging sand at another child in a sandbox. Before you get mad or assign blame, take a breath and ask your partner for his or her perspective. You can change your relationship for the better by increasing the use of some statements, such as "I love you," "I'm here for you," "I understand," "I'm sorry," "Thank you," "I really appreciate all that you do," "It's so nice to see you," and "That was quite an accomplishment!" Leave gratitude in love notes, hide them so they will find them, or look deeply into their eyes and tell them. Be creative! A compliment is a sign of acknowledgement and appreciation. Make an effort to affirm your spouse's value in life and in love.

When you take responsibility for your part in the marriage, only then will you be able to connect with your partner in a mature, intimate way.

Also, inform them about learning how to agree and disagree. No two people agree on everything, and that's okay, but it's important to be okay with each other's differences. In order to strengthen your marriage, learn to recognize that most arguments have shared responsibility, that both people have valid points and valid reasons for their feelings.

If you argue with your partner, drop the shaming, blaming, needing to be right and really listen without interrupting. Then communicate how you feel, using the "I" statements.

It's not your partner's job to read your mind, guess what you are thinking, or put words into your mouth. Every time you open your mouth to complain about something, whether it's the food, the service, the movie, the weather, etc., these are huge obstacles to open, honest communication, and will guarantee resentment, anger, and frustration in the relationship.

In the heat of the moment, what feels super-important will likely fade in importance as time goes by. Before you react by yelling, tossing insults or unkind words, remember that "This too, shall pass." So, don't let one unfortunate incident, difficult argument or challenging moment destroy your lifetime of happiness.

One day, my Mother told me a story that always come back into my mind whenever a person annoys me and I feel like giving that person a piece of my mind. After realizing that what I may say will not get the situation any better, rather may worsen it, that's when I remember that my mom told me that her mother (my Grandma, RIP), every time she got into an argument with Grandpa (RIP), she could run and drool water, in order to prevent saying a word to him which would make my grandpa angry and put them into a fight. It's so easy to get sucked into the drama of fighting with your significant other. And while it may feel easier to just be angry and upset with them, simply changing your mindset about the situation can do wonders.

Choosing to ignore pleasure and turn to living in stress and chaos can, over time, severely damage your marriage. The unprocessed emotions and unspoken words generated in stressful moments can diminish pleasure and leave your marriage dried and dying for attention. Choosing stress can alter your intimacy and put walls around your heart, making you inaccessible to love. Arguing with your spouse can get ugly really quick if you are not careful.

Rather than lash out at each other with insults, try clearly communicating what's bothering you and how you want the situation to be resolved. Marriage isn't easy, and it's normal for partners to get upset with each other occasionally. But if you make small adjustments in the right way, they could lead to big results.

When it gets hard in a relationship, our tendency is to protect ourselves, to retreat, to "lean out." Leaning out when your partner reaches out creates distance and dissonance. If instead you "lean in" to the uncomfortable feelings, to the unknown and your own vulnerability, and meet your partner, you can actually strengthen your relationship through the struggles you face together. When your partner tells you something (about you) that is bothering him or her, reflect back what he is saying. When you "mirror", that will help you not feel as defensive and will allow you the opportunity to better understand what your partner is trying to communicate.

Do everything you can to support your partner's well-being and respect your partner. One of the most important factors in a good marriage is respect. Respect each other, avoid verbal abuse, and keep insults to yourself. Bad words are just like squeezing toothpaste out of its tube, once it is out, you can never get it back in again. It is much easier to create your best relationship together if both people's needs are voiced, heard and supported by their partner.

Some part of your partner feels he is falling because you aren't having a great time. Men are happiest when they can please their women. Save the full critique for your girlfriends and in the meantime, let him see the best in you.

Communication and time together are the keys to strengthening your marriage. Impossible to imagine one without the other! If you live with your partner or see each other once in a while due to today's globalization that made people work miles away from their homes, communication is essential. Couples often lose each other because of their busy lives— work, children, computers, and separate male/female activities. A healthy marriage is one that has a mix of individual, family, and couple time. The amount of each may be different for each couple, but the mix is necessary to keep a functional marriage. Focus on what there is to appreciate about your mate, then honestly and spontaneously express your specific appreciation to him or her. It's also good to do this for yourself. It's really good loving your marriage by first taking care of yourself. If you keep working on you, your marriage will stay fresh and vital. Promise to take care of yourself so you will continue to age with grace and confidence by your partner's side.

If your spouse treats you with kindness, gentleness, patience, and self-control, it's easy for you to respond kindly. If you are treated badly, with anger, impatience, etc., it's difficult to be nice in return. Focus on how you can be a blessing to your spouse and in turn, you will be blessed and so will your marriage.

The best way to strengthen a marriage is to support and assist each other in being the best you can be. A strong marriage is one in which both people understand that the other person needs to have outside interests and activities which help them to feel happy and fulfilled. A strong marriage is one where both people understand that it is more important to be happy than it is to be right.

Put also the following into consideration:

- Keep at what you believe in and realize that there will always be days and people who will want to hold you down.

- Be a better parent than your parents. Stop bad cycles and habits. Always try to be better yourself.

- Enter and stay in a relationship for the right reasons. True love is about affection, selflessness, and generosity.

- You can't get respect unless you first give it. And that goes for not just significant others but also friends and family. Model the respect you seek in a partner.

- If you test someone, he may fail you. Don't administer litmus tests as measures of a person's love. Testing is a sign of one's own fear and insecurity.

For men, it's important to understand that women want to be listened to. Men don't need to solve or fix everything; listening itself is an exceptional gift. A woman needs her partner to spend time giving her his full attention and looking directly into her eyes. When she receives this, she can easily get in touch with her feelings of love for her husband and becomes much more receptive to his needs. This is how intimacy can be fulfilling for both people…magical even!

While writing this, I remembered sometime back when my husband and I were about to be engaged. We were together in a Chinese city called Guangzhou. He held my arms, looked into my eyes (my big eyes) and told me to listen to the song he was about to play. That song was a song by Bryan Adams, called "To really love a woman". He talked about how much he loves me and that he saw his unborn children in my eyes! (That was his way of informing me that he wanted me to be the mother of his future children). That song has the words that indeed touched my heart till now. And I'm sure no woman wouldn't like to hear such words (followed by actions) from her lover boy.

For women, it's important to understand that men need time for themselves. By giving him space to pull away and not taking it personally, you allow him to reconnect with his desire for you and his commitment to the relationship. Create regular opportunities for fun, laughter, and positive experiences. Figure out what communicates love to each other and do that. Be observant and thoughtful with little things and even do chores that the other dislikes. Consciously doing what opens and softens your spouse's heart will benefit you both in the long run and keep your marriage happier. Setting aside a romantic evening on a regular basis can rekindle the magic of a long-term relationship. It doesn't have to be fancy, just special time for the two of you to remember how and why you first fell in love.

With today's hectic schedules, it's easy to find your marriage at the bottom of the priority list. Take a walk and hold hands (nature calms), couple-cook (food fight), exercise together (tennis or maybe dancing), or just collect a "Daily Joke" to share. It doesn't have to be expensive, but if you make the commitment and effort to laugh together as often as possible, it can sweeten your connection and cement your relationship for life.

Treat the following with every possible remedy you have got:

- Boredom in the bedroom, lack of conversations, and resentment. These are symptoms and they need to be treated just as you would treat a chronic illness that seemingly has no cure. Throw at them every possible remedy you have got, no matter how alternative or weird it seems. Chances are one or more of them will actually work and your marriage will get stronger and stronger.

- Never turn your husband down for making love. He won't go anywhere else if he is fed well at home.

- Be playful, make it fun and keep it interesting. Our body deserves pleasure. Our bodies aren't just objects to be pursued and desired by our partners. They are ours to enjoy, explore and feel experiences fully.

- Be kind and sweet. Never cut him down in front of people, especially your children. This will hurt him deeper than anything. Let him have his male pride even when you think he is wrong.

- Hold your tongue. It's better to be loved than to be right.

- Allow him to do his job-lead, provide and protect you in the best way he knows how. Don't stand in his way or rise up against him. Be honest and say anything you want to say but in a respectful manner. This will get you a long way.

- Children learn disobedience, dishonesty and disregard from their mother's example toward their father. Stand by him when he disciplines your children. Never pick them up or cuddle them after punishment until they have made up with their father.

- Uphold his rules and leadership of the family. Remember he has veto power in all decisions. Never disagree with him in front of the children. Present a united front. You can voice your concerns at a more private time.

When it comes to making a marriage last and being successful, the most important thing to focus on is effort. You can't expect change to happen if both partners aren't willing to try new things and new ways of thinking. If you rely on old, toxic behaviors to handle arguments and stressful situations, then you will just find yourself in the same repetitive patterns over and over again. It's time to break the cycle and show your partner some love. Last but not least, always try to be affectionate towards your partner, no matter how long you guys will be together. If you play your part well, the rest will take care of itself. And if it doesn't, at least your hands and heart will be clean, and you will have the peace of mind.

PARENTS' WRONG ADVISE

Parenting includes consciously helping children grow into happy and secure individuals, individuals who can extend themselves in relationships and share their lives harmoniously and lovingly with their life partners. But more often, parents inadvertently raise their children to be selfish, suspicious and insecure. They do so by often modelling such traits themselves, and sometimes even consciously and verbally teaching them to distrust their spouse. Wait a minute, before you tell your daughter to never trust her husband, how do you ensure that other drivers stay in their lanes, hence, giving you the confidence to drive comfortably in your own. Do you sleep in the aircraft and wait for somebody to announce your arrival somewhere? Do you cook all your food? Who pumps water into your house? Where do you keep your money? Do you accept anesthesia for a surgical operation? Trust is a lifestyle!

Sometimes, parents are insecure themselves, either because of an unhappy marriage, sickness, or financial concerns.

There are parents who, when they do not get along with their daughter in-law, a good girl that their son is pleased with, tell their son to divorce his wife. There are parents who are insecure in their old age and whenever a visitor comes to see them, complain about how their offspring with their spouses fall short in fulfilling their rights. The parent's role in marrying off their children is manifested in giving advice, direction, and guidance. Marriage is one of a person's private affairs. Family is the essential building block of society, and upon this sound basis, civilization is established and values are elevated.

Over-protectiveness

This is the constant support of over-protective parents and bending over backwards to re-arrange the world for the comfort of their children, and they do not have faith in their child to be able to tap into his inner resources to help himself. Children of such parents lack faith in themselves and their own capabilities and remain psychologically dependent on their parents. They keep turning to their parents for every problem, including problems in their marriage, expecting them to 'fix" things as always. The parents' over-protectiveness and making life "easy" for their child at all times leave the child ill-equipped to think in his own interest. It may cause the child being incapable of choosing wisely, make confident decisions, and take actions to live a fulfilling and happy life.

Interference & Undue Demands

Some parents interfere with sensitive issues in their married children's lives such as their sexual relationships with their partners.

I have heard about a young couple where the wife was dissatisfied with the reduced intimacy with her husband. This left her increasingly frustrated. She unwittingly rented her frustration with her mother, and that was the beginning of the end of her marriage. Her mother confronted her son-in-law. She accused him of hiding his "sexual weakness".

Being perfectly potent, this allegation was unacceptable. The bitterness between the couple increased so much that they broke off all communication and ended separating legally. This shows how parents can ruin a child's marriage. If parents cannot free their children to be happy and give happiness to their spouses, they have failed in their role as parents. It's their moral duty to model genuinely mutually respectful relationships as a couple for their children.

They are also those parents who often influence their children by showing their disapproval when they don't get their way with their children's spouses. This creates disharmony between couples.

When parents expect their children's partner to fall in line with their valid or invalid demands, they sow the seed of trouble between the couple. As the children pressure their spouses to please their parents and get their approval, marriages start crumbling under such pressures.

WHEN A COUPLE BECOMES THREE

Children will change almost everything no matter how much you promise each other they won't. When a couple becomes three or more, life changes. You can't have a tiny, stinky, loud, crying, hungry, fussy human being, who will never let you sleep as you used to, living in your house and nothing changes. You will have to find your new normal as parents, not just a married couple. You will not be out partying in the hottest clubs in designer clothes anymore. While the birth of a baby brings great joy into a couple's life, it is also taxing on any relationship. The first few weeks can be overwhelming, especially for new parents. The world revolves around coping with little sleep, twenty-four-hour care, hormonal changes, breastfeeding issues and financial concerns.

Although the birth of a baby can be overwhelming, there is also an intense intimacy shared between two parents when they look at the baby they share. Turning your twosome, a threesome is bound to alter your relationship. The gift of a baby can add an intense intimacy within a relationship. However, difficulties may surface when a couple only functions as a threesome and ignores the vital importance of the twosome.

So even though you need to strive to be the best parents to your child, you are also a couple and you need to nurture your relationship with your partner.

Some things **should** not be shared

Well, you love your partner, and he/she loves you too, but who really wants his/her partner to show how much ear wax he just cleaned out? Do you think it's alright showing him how you can pop a zit with one hand? Hell no!! Close the bathroom door. We all know what is going on, but no one wants to see or smell it. It's not that you will be ashamed or embarrassed, but it's a matter of privacy. This isn't about shame or pretending you are perfect or hiding things from each other, it's about keeping the mystery going. He doesn't need to see you changing a tampon. But if you are sick or hurt or need help with any of these stuffs, that's different.

Few other things couples need to keep in mind:

There will be extremely difficult days in your marriage where you will question your own choice as a spouse. Do not take important decisions regarding your marriage on such days. Such days are meant for letting your mind go blank, not for taking decisions which you are bound to regret later on.

- Your husband/wife will not be the only man/woman on this planet. Go out, meet people, make friends.

- Communication is the foundation to a happy, healthy, long-lasting marriage. Your expectations stay inside your brain and there is no way another person can know them. Learn to communicate.

- Be sensitive to your spouse's emotions. If you don't have an emotional quotient, grow it. Without realizing what your spouse is going through, you can't have a happy marriage.

- Delegate responsibilities and jobs, such as paying bills.

- Your spouse is the person you share your life with. He/she is not the same person as you and does not have the same life as yours. Do not interfere with his/her choices unless they are screwing up your life. That's the minimum amount of respect you can have for another human being.

- Get rid of gender roles. Your spouse isn't supposed to do a particular thing just because he is a man or just because she is a woman. Do things together if possible, and if not, the person who is in a position to do the work should do it, irrespective of gender.

- Your marriage can be a fairy tale if you make it that.

- Love can always be there if you allow it. Marriage is not about what you can get, but what you can give. Marriages can survive a lot of bumpy times and be made stronger.

- You are not always right.

- Enjoy each other, before and after children (if there are to be any).

- Your spouse can be your best friend for life.

- Remember the little notes or silly texts

- Remember the important dates

- Buy spontaneous gifts for no reason

- Money pressures and other challenges are all temporary. Sometimes there is a string of pressures, but they can be handled one by one.

- Remember often why you fell in love with your spouse. Build on that.

- Consult with each other on important decisions. You will deal with another person's issues, events, etc., even when you do not like it.

- You must become financially responsible. A married couple should not spend money lavishly and becomes a burden to the society or else the ultimate purpose of marriage is spoiled.

- Now you will be sharing a household and managing it is a job for the both of you.

- Love is not just a feeling; it is a choice. In any long-term relationship, that feeling will come and go at times. It's a choice to love the other person and to consistently take actions that will keep the relationship going.

- Marriage was never meant to be a power struggle. It was meant to be a power union.

- The deeper you dig, the more chances of finding gold. Try again a bit harder!

- God cares about your marriage. Don't leave Him out of it.

REFERENCES

- Discourses of Brigham Young, sel. John A. Windtsoe, Salt Lake City: Desert Book co.,1941
- The teachings of Spencer W. Kimball, ed. Edward L. Kimball, Salt Lake City:Bookcraft,1982, p.31
- The Holly Bible, Proverbs 22:6 (King James Version)
- Mind in the making by Ellen Gainssky
- Fun on the run, by Cynthia L. Copeland
- "Have You Ever Really Loved A Woman" by Bryan Adams

www.ingramcontent.com/pod-product-compliance
Lightning Source LLC
Chambersburg PA
CBHW070611010526
44118CB00012B/1487